APART AT THE SEAMS

APART AT THE SEAMS

THE COLLAPSE OF PRIVATE PENSION AND HEALTH CARE PROTECTIONS

Charles R. Morris

A CENTURY FOUNDATION REPORT

The Century Foundation Press • New York

√

The Century Foundation sponsors and supervises timely analyses of economic policy, foreign affairs, and domestic political issues. Not-for-profit and nonpartisan, it was founded in 1919 and endowed by Edward A. Filene.

LIBRARY OF CONGRESS CATALOGING-IN-PUBLICATION DATA

Morris, Charles R.
Apart at the seams: the collapse of private pension and health care protections / Charles R. Morris.
    p. cm.
"A Century Foundation Report."
Includes bibliographical references and index.
ISBN 0-87078-501-X (pbk. : alk. paper)
    1. Pensions—United States. 2. Employer-sponsored health insurance—United States. 3. Social security—United States. 4. Medicaid. 5. Employee fringe benefits—United States. 6. Corporations—United States—Finance. I. Title.
HD7125.M64 2006
331.25'20973—dc22

2005036371

Cover design and illustration by Claude Goodwin.

Manufactured in the United States of America.

FOREWORD

For nearly fifty years, the postwar baby-boom generation of Americans has had a dramatic impact on the culture, economy, tastes, and public policies of the nation. Now, as the boomers approach their final act—old age—the challenges of providing retirement security and health care for the nation's aging population have been increasingly setting the terms of domestic political debate. President George W. Bush's campaign to modify the Social Security system is only one example of this phenomenon. The president's approach has foundered in great part because its reliance on private accounts would place the average worker's pension and disability benefits at much greater risk. Congress and the public, wisely we believe, have refused to allow such basic social insurance provisions to be at the mercy of the ups and downs of the stock market.

Apparent success in preserving Social Security, however, should not obscure the greatly heightened risk that pervades the rest of the American social insurance system. The United States, in marked contrast to virtually every other advanced industrial economy, depends heavily on employers to provide health insurance and old-age pensions to their workers. In most other countries, the government guarantees that all citizens are entitled to medical insurance and requires employers to pay for retirement benefits. Our social insurance system, however, relies mainly on tax incentives to encourage employers to take responsibility for their workers' health insurance and pensions. That approach always has been far from perfect, with large segments of the population lacking any protections whatsoever because many employers decide the tax breaks are not a sufficient inducement. But in recent years, the gaps in coverage have steadily widened and the reliability of protections, even at the most generous companies, has eroded severely.

As recently as 1980, about 83 percent of large- and medium-sized companies offered defined benefit pension plans, which provide guaranteed retirement benefits based on past salary and years of service. By 2003, only 33 percent of large employers provided such plans, as many companies switched to defined contribution plans whose payments ultimately depend on investment performance. Even the defined benefit plans that remain are not as guaranteed as they used to be. Many companies have gone bankrupt with inadequately funded retirement plans—so many, in fact, that the quasi-public agency responsible for insuring private pension benefits (the Pension Benefit Guarantee Corporation) is itself threatened with bankruptcy.

Private firms are rapidly cutting back on medical insurance, too. General Motors and Ford are the most visible among the many companies that are telling their workers and retirees that health care spending must be cut if the company is to survive. That means individuals are paying higher premiums and copayments while in many cases receiving less extensive coverage. The same trends have extended to the governmental health insurance programs of Medicare and Medicaid.

No author is better qualified to explain how and why the U.S. social insurance system is shifting more and more risk onto the shoulders of individual Americans than Charles R. Morris. Author of two previous Century Foundation books, Morris has held a number of important positions, including serving as a managing partner of a consulting firm specializing in the financial services and investment banking industries and as secretary of health and human services for the state of Washington. He also is the author of a number of critically acclaimed books.

In this publication, Morris succinctly describes the historical roots of the idiosyncratic U.S. social insurance system and the forces that are causing it to unravel. He also describes the features of today's economic and political environment that have, in Morris' words, "conspired to create an unusually unpromising environment for meaningful reform."

The public policy responses needed to halt the breakdown of our social insurance system are not clear, and Morris does not presume to have a belt full of silver bullets. What his analysis makes brilliantly clear is that we do not simply have a Social Security problem or a health care problem: our current retirement and health care provision and financing systems will not survive in the long run. The policy challenge is not simply to pay for Social Security (a fairly manageable task) or to shift the burden from the public and private sectors onto families. Instead, we must decide how to strengthen protections for citizens against a range of financial risks in an age of globalization and rapid technological change.

The challenges connected to the aging of the population during a period of rising economic inequality have been central to The Century Foundation's agenda for years. In addition to explanatory pamphlets and analytical issue briefs available on our Web site, www.tcf.org, we have published a number of books and reports on this issue. On Social Security, those publications include *Countdown to Reform: The Great Social Security Debate* by Henry J. Aaron and Robert D. Reischauer, Robert M. Ball's *Insuring the Essentials* and *Straight Talk About Social Security,* Robert Eisner's *Social Security: More Not Less,* Joseph White's *False Alarm,* and *Beyond the Basics: Social Security Reform,* a volume edited by Richard C. Leone and Greg Anrig, Jr. On health insurance, we have published a task force report, *Medicare Tomorrow;* Leif Wellington Haase's *A New Deal for Health;* and Eliot Fishman's *Running in Place: How the Medicaid Model Falls Short and What to Do about It.*

The first step in solving this problem surely is to understand it. With this book, Charles Morris lifts us above the piecemeal, partisan analysis typical of these issues and permits us to see the grander picture. The options we confront are not simple, but with the help of this book, we will understand them much more clearly.

RICHARD C. LEONE, *President*
The Century Foundation
January 2006

CONTENTS

FOREWORD *by Richard C. Leone*   v

1. INTRODUCTION   1

2. HOW WE GOT HERE   7

3. A SYSTEM UNDER STRESS   13

4. RECENT TRENDS IN INCOME, DEBT, AND WEALTH
   IN THE UNITED STATES   31

5. THE SPECIAL CASE OF HEALTH CARE   39

6. THE ROCKY PATH TO REFORM   55

NOTES   61

INDEX   69

ABOUT THE AUTHOR   75

1

INTRODUCTION

Few public policy issues are as consequential as the reform of the United States' retirement and health insurance systems. Publicly provided systems are under severe financial pressure precisely at a time when employers are rapidly withdrawing from the provision of traditional health and retirement benefits. The consequence is great gaps in coverage—far worse than in any other industrial nation—that place tens of millions of people at risk. Since an abundance of reform proposals have been generated from across the political spectrum, the purpose of this report is not to produce yet another proposal, but to throw light on some of the historical, economic, and political realities that must be taken into account for any reform to be successful.

THE PROBLEM

Although the financial difficulties of America's public retirement and health care systems—predominantly Social Security and Medicare/Medicaid—are well known, far less attention has been paid to the parallel collapse of private sector retirement and health insurance systems.

1

Throughout most of the last century, America, uniquely among industrial countries, assumed that private businesses would take primary responsibility for providing retirement security and health insurance to working-age people and their families—an arrangement that became known as American "welfare capitalism." The question of whether citizens' retirement and health care would be provided primarily by the state, or primarily by business, was one of the hardest-fought political battles of the New Deal. The final compromise accepted a federally operated Social Security system, but one expressly designed to supplement employer-based plans, while reserving health insurance provision to employers. It was another thirty years before Medicare and Medicaid were established for the aged and the very poor, who were not likely to be covered by employer-based programs.

By 1980, some 83 percent of large and medium-sized companies offered so-called defined benefit pension plans (which provide guaranteed retirement income based on years of service and previous salary) while virtually all companies provided health care coverage for full-time employees and their families.[1] Indeed, until relatively recently it was normal for larger companies to maintain their employees' health insurance coverage even after they became eligible for Medicare.

The success of the welfare capitalist model obscured the degree to which it depended on the global dominance of American business. For most of the twentieth century, the American business environment was characterized by tight oligopolistic control by a few leading companies in most key industries. Prices were "administered" rather than strictly competitive, and there was great stability in lifetime employment relationships.

Those core assumptions were destroyed by the fierce competitive onslaught launched by foreign companies on almost every major American industry in the 1970s and 1980s. In the new world of global competition, prices are dictated by iron laws of marginalist economics, old traditions of employer-employee loyalties are a distant memory, and companies are shedding benefit commitments as rapidly as possible.

By 2003, the percentage of large private employers offering defined benefit pension plans had dropped to only 33 percent (and to 9 percent among smaller employers). Only 58 percent of private employers offered any health insurance coverage, and those that did were offloading more and more of the costs onto their employees.[2] More than half of the working age Americans without health insurance had full-time jobs throughout the survey year, but their employers either did not offer coverage or offered it at rates employees could not afford.[3]

The policy question, in short, is no longer *whether* a private-sector benefit system is an adequate solution, but how to fill the gap left by its disappearance.

THE POLICY ENVIRONMENT

The policy challenges of restructuring core systems of retirement and health care provision are daunting. Unique features of the current economic and political environment, however, have conspired to create an unusually unpromising environment for meaningful reform. Consider, for example:

◆   The historic demographic shift triggered by the aging of the baby boomers—about a fifth of the population will be aged sixty-five-plus for many decades to come. Regardless of how it is accomplished, very large financial reallocations to support boomers' retirement and health care needs are unavoidable.

◆   An unusually fractious political arena, and the disappearance of a bipartisan congressional centrist "party," like the one that mediated the 1983 Social Security financial reforms.

◆   The deliberate compression of the federal tax base under the Bush administration—federal taxes as a percent of GDP are now the lowest since the Eisenhower era[4]—accompanied by very heavy military and pork-barrel spending.

◆   The extraordinary absorption of economic gains by the very richest American households. During 2003, for example, the bottom 99 percent of earners lost ground to inflation, while a quarter of all income gains were captured by the top one-tenth of 1 percent of earners.[5]

◆   The rickety balance sheets of American households and the explosion of sub-prime consumer lending. An unusually large share of household debt is at floating rates, much of it secured by housing equity, which sharpens vulnerability to interest rate rises and/or a cooling of the housing bull market.

◆   Aspects of American health care that lead to unusually high costs, largely as a consequence of the design biases of an employer-managed benefits regime.

THE NEAR-TERM PROSPECT

Despite a proliferation of solution outlines from both liberal and conservative policy institutes, none appears to command the consensus required for major reform in the United States. At the same time, current policy biases are perversely tilted to make things worse, especially with respect to health care. The conservatives who control both the White House and the Congress have proved highly receptive to powerful business interests, and health care is now one of the country's largest industries. The new Medicare prescription drug program, for example, seems almost calculated to be very expensive and highly profitable to the insurance and pharmaceutical industries. At the same time, there has been a quiet, but steady, expansion of tax-supported health care, as state Medicaid programs expand to cover lower-income workers without access to private coverage.

The near-term prospect, therefore, is for continued rapid, spastic growth in public sector retirement and health insurance spending. How long that can continue without a top-to-bottom restructuring is likely to be determined by outside forces, like the attractiveness of American debt instruments in world capital markets. In light of current political divisions, however, it may take a truly catastrophic crisis to galvanize broad reform.

DESIGN OF THE REPORT

The report is not intended to develop detailed reform proposals, but rather to help clarify the context for reformist agendas. It will therefore present:

◆   a short history of the evolution of the American benefit system;

◆   an overview of the current state of both the government and private-sector retirement and health benefit systems;

◆   a snapshot of American household income, debt, and savings;

◆   a brief analysis of fundamental forces driving continued expansion of the health care sector; and finally,

◆   a short list of likely feature-sets required for enduring reform.

2

HOW WE GOT HERE

Yale University political scientist Jacob Hacker points out that national dispensations for retirement and health benefits, like all complex systems, evolve in a way that is "path-dependent."[1] Where you start from crucially limits the choices of where you can go, and at each stage of the process, quasi-intentional micro-choices accumulate into impassable points of no return.

THE ORIGINS

During the first three-quarters of the twentieth century, the American system of benefit provision took shape within an institutional landscape dominated by a remarkably stable and long-lived cadre of big companies. The firms that won leadership in steel, oil, aluminum, telephony, railroads, chemicals, electrical appliances, food processing, banking, and retail distribution before World War I mostly held their positions into the 1980s. New industries like automobiles, aircraft, and radio and television reshuffled the company rankings from time to time, but they all evolved along the same stable oligopolistic pattern followed by their older brethren. The top American firms were already globally dominant by the early 1900s, and by the 1950s, after two world wars, the competitive positions of most of the bigger American companies seemed unassailable. Although the majority of American workers did not work at the biggest firms, big-company employment policies filtered down to the thousands of smaller businesses that were their suppliers and customers. By the mid-1950s, big companies and big industrial unions put aside the bitter confrontations of the 1930s and 1940s, and labor relations settled into a comparatively strife-free sharing of the economic pie.[2]

The institutional poverty of government reinforced business dominance. The minimalist federal government of the pre-Depression era foreclosed any hopes of Bismarckian-style social insurance, while the diversity of state politics posed an insuperable bar to alternative forms of coordinated national solutions. A 1920s Progressive initiative for state-based universal health care collapsed in the face of a concerted business threat to relocate plants away from any jurisdiction imposing compulsory benefit standards. Finally, a remarkable bout of post–World War I anti-Bolshevik hysteria—the "Red Scare"—virtually doomed any program with even a whiff of "socialism." The American Medical Association (AMA), which was just then becoming the primary political voice for physicians, took anti-collectivism to the extreme of opposing even private health insurance or business provision of health care benefits.

Business was not entirely unresponsive. Even before World War I, the "Social Gospel" movement and the interest of a new cadre of professional managers in improving productivity and combating unionism focused attention on worker welfare. The railroads, along with leading industrial companies like GE, Dupont, and Westinghouse, were among the early movers. Employer-sponsored benefit systems came to be dubbed American "welfare capitalism." Early benefits tended to concentrate on training and safety, group life insurance, and limited pension provision for long-time employees, like railroad engineers, whom companies wished to encourage to retire for safety and other reasons. "Personnel" became an established profession, and a number of companies began to hire female personnel officers, frequently with training in social work.[3] Worker benefits, however, were rarely vested and were often managed capriciously—pro-union activity might cost a worker his pension.

Health care benefits were rare until the 1920s, and first became common in industries like autos and steel to counter unionizing pressures. Commercial insurers in search of products to complement their group life businesses added to the push for group health benefits. Hospitals and physicians countered the commercial insurers' drive with their Blue Cross and Blue Shield plans, respectively, usually with legislated protections and privileges in their home states. The attractiveness of employer-provided benefits increased when Congress overrode Treasury objections to establish the full tax-deductibility of virtually all employee benefits in 1926.

THE NEW DEAL

A spike in antibusiness sentiment during the Great Depression offered a fleeting opportunity to create a national social insurance system. While some leading welfare capitalists like GE's Gerard Swope and Kodak's Marion Folsom supported the New Deal initiatives, the mainstream business lobbies and their congressional allies remained strongly opposed to federal social insurance of any kind. After business lobbies almost won a killer amendment to make Social Security participation voluntary, the administration decided to defer national health insurance to concentrate on Social Security and unemployment compensation. Big losses in the 1938 congressional elections killed any chances of winning health insurance in Roosevelt's second term; very soon in any case, in Roosevelt's words, "Doctor New Deal" was replaced by "Doctor Win the War." Alarmed by its narrow escape, the American Medical Association dropped its opposition to voluntary health insurance (provided that traditional fee-for-service payment practices were preserved), and a strong constituency quickly developed behind the burgeoning Blue Cross/Blue Shield and other private insurance arrangements.

Business opposition to Social Security waned as it gradually dawned that federal old-age insurance allowed managers to introduce pension systems only for their upper-stratum employees. One 37,500-strong employer typified the reaction. A spokesman pointed out that only 1,200 of its employees had any managerial role, all of them with salaries over $3,000, "So we decided that we will have nothing paid into the [company pension] plan by either employer or employee on salaries below $3,000, and we will let the social-security-tax program take care of the salaries under $3,000."[4]

THE HALCYON YEARS

The big-company-centered boom that followed upon American's entry into the war clinched the victory of welfare capitalism. From the Depression year of 1938 to the peak of war production in 1944, national output doubled.[5] The prevalent cost-plus system of military contracting left companies rolling in cash, even as wartime wage freezes and high corporate tax rates provided a powerful incentive toward benefit expansion. Between 1940 and 1950, the share of civilian workers covered by private pensions rose from about 7 percent to nearly 20 percent, while the coverage of private health insurance rose from 10 percent to 50 percent. Few pundits were surprised when President Truman's plan for national health insurance was summarily dismissed by a hostile Congress. The Republican victory in 1952, and Eisenhower's choice of Kodak's Folsom as HEW secretary, underscored the preeminence of the welfare capitalist model. Unions jumped on the bandwagon as they recognized the bargaining opportunity in employer-run benefit systems. Between 1948 and 1954, the number of workers covered by collectively bargained health plans jumped tenfold, to 27 million. In the pension arena, craft-oriented unions, like the Teamsters and those in the building trades, created their own union pension funds, further eroding support for national solutions.

The 1950s were welfare capitalism's golden age. The United States, with just 6 percent of global population, disposed of roughly half the world's production, and an even larger share of world income and financial resources. Unionized workers became accustomed to noncontributory health and welfare plans, productivity bonuses, and annual cost-of-living increases, while corporate executives savored their cigars at company-sponsored golf clubs. The percentage of workers with health and pension benefits rose sharply through the 1960s, before gradually reaching a high point in the early 1980s, when about 40 percent of all workers were covered by private pension plans, and nearly 80 percent had private health insurance.[6] At the same time, however, since employee benefits were for the most part under control of company managers, they were deliberately skewed to reinforce company recruitment and retention objectives. In 1990, for example, about 57 percent of all workplace pension benefits flowed to the wealthiest fifth of households.[7]

Good times even defanged conservative opposition to Social Security. From the late 1950s through the 1960s, Social Security benefits were steadily increased, until the Nixon administration indexed them to wage inflation in 1973. (Nixon may have viewed that as a *defensive* measure, to impose some cap on the benefit bidding wars that regularly broke out in the Congress.) Proposals for a unified national health insurance program were not seriously aired again until the 1990s, although the Johnson administration, over bitter AMA opposition, managed to pass the Medicare and Medicaid programs in 1965. The selling point for both programs was that they were carefully targeted at the elderly and the poor left behind by welfare capitalism. The AMA's philosophic opposition to government health care finally gave way before the prospect of a financial windfall. Both programs incorporated a more or less open-ended commitment to providers' "usual and customary" fee protocols, and physicians' incomes rose dramatically.

The Great Unravelling

The collapse of America's industrial preeminence in the 1970s and 1980s invalidated the fundamental premises of American welfare capitalism. The onslaught of Japanese and European companies on global manufacturing and technology markets exposed

America's proudest companies—AT&T, U.S. Steel, General Motors—as sclerotic, out-of-touch bureaucracies.[8] As American companies frantically retooled and reorganized through the 1980s and 1990s, their recovery was dangerously undermined by their welfare capitalist legacy. Forced retirement programs came with crushing pension and retiree health costs even as the decades of open-ended health insurance provision touched off a vast, and very expensive, technological reshaping of the health care industry. The murkiness of benefits accounting obscured the depth of the problem for many years, but the focus on corporate reporting in the past decade has cast a pitiless light on company vulnerabilities. Health care liabilities at American automobile companies, just for *retirees,* add somewhere between $800 and $1,300 to the cost of each car, depending on who is counting.[9] At the same time, the new companies that have sprung up to lead an American recovery are extremely wary of the kind of long-term employment commitment that was a presupposition of the welfare capitalist model.

The question, therefore, is not whether the American social insurance system must be fundamentally restructured. That has been going on, willy-nilly, for the past twenty years. In the new world of global competitiveness, with radically reduced business capacity to support the old welfare capitalist dispensation, the question is: Are there reasonable paths to closing the gaping holes in the existing system, without doing violence to the long-standing American disposition toward mixed-enterprise solutions?

3

A SYSTEM UNDER STRESS

Retirement and health provision in the United States are built around four primary programs. Two of them are federal: Social Security—officially, Old-Age, Survivors, and Disability Insurance (OASDI)—and Medicare/Medicaid. Medicare and Medicaid are aimed at different target populations, but there are many overlaps, most notably in the financing of nursing home and home health care for seniors. The second two are the private sector, employer-sponsored, retirement and health insurance systems. Since the categorical restrictions on the federal programs exclude most working-age people and their families, the majority of Americans rely on employer-sponsored benefits in the welfare capitalist tradition.

The four primary programs account for the dominant portion of what analysts call American "social insurance"—which would also include food stamps, unemployment compensation, the earned income tax credit, and similar programs. Perhaps surprisingly, within the recent past, the total social insurance provision as a share of U.S. GDP has been roughly at the norm for other major industrial countries. OECD economists have analyzed total social insurance spending in major countries, using 1995 data (see Figures 3.1 and 3.2, page 15), including both public and "private social" spending.[1] ("Private social" spending is managed by nonpublic entities, such as employers, but is regulated or subsidized through favorable taxation or other measures.) The spending calculations also include "tax expenditures" such as employer tax deductions for worker benefits.* (The value of federal tax expenditures for private sector pensions and health insurance is estimated at more than $250 billion in 2005, or nearly as much as the total Medicare budget.[2]) Over the sample of thirteen countries, the share of GDP dedicated to social insurance spending was tightly clustered, consuming about a quarter of national resources everywhere, despite considerable variation in financing and taxation mechanisms.

The United States, with 24.5 percent of its GDP devoted to social insurance, according to the OECD analysts, was exactly in the median position of the countries in the sample. The top spender in the sample, Germany, devoted 27.7 percent of GDP to social insurance, so the gap between the median and top position was modest.**

The question, then, is why are there are such gaping holes in the American social insurance system? Why do so many workers have only minimal protection for retirement income and, often, no health care coverage at all. The answer, in part, is because the United States relies to such a great extent on its crumbling "private social" system. The share of private social provision in U.S. social insurance is more than twice as high as in the next highest country, and more than four times the median. The next two sections briefly review the present state of the American public and private retirement and health insurance systems.

---

* Tax expenditures are properly included in the data since a reduction in normal tax revenue to encourage a specific activity is fiscally equivalent to an increase in government spending for that activity. The OECD analysts, however, omitted tax breaks for private pensions, because of the difficulty of constructing comparable data sets.
** The lowest ranking country, Ireland, at only 18.7 percent, is a demographic outlier, since emigration has left it with a young workforce and modest social insurance obligations.

Figure 3.1. Comparative Social Insurance Spending (as percent of GDP), Including "Private Social" Spending—OECD Countries, 1995

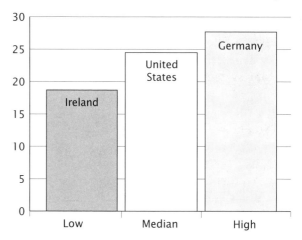

Source: William Adema, "Net Social Expenditure," *Labour Market and Social Policy—Occasional Papers No. 39* (Paris: OECD, August 1999), Table 7.

Figure 3.2. "Private Social" Spending as Percent of GDP—OECD Countries, 1995

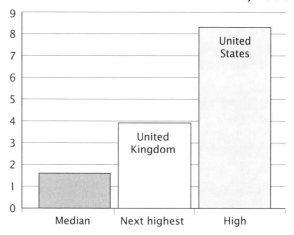

Source: William Adema, "Net Social Expenditure," *Labour Market and Social Policy—Occasional Papers No. 39* (Paris: OECD, August 1999), Table 7.

THE SHAPE OF THE CRISIS I: THE FEDERAL SYSTEMS

SOCIAL SECURITY

Ironically, despite the concerted focus of the Bush administration on "saving" Social Security though privatization, it is the least under stress of the four systems. Social Security is financed by payroll taxes—currently 12.4 percent on the first $90,000 of earnings, divided equally between employers and employees. Financing is primarily pay-as-you-go with an actuarial overlay. A major payroll tax increase in 1983 generated a surplus of payroll tax collections over annual outlays; by law the surpluses are invested in special issues of ten-year Treasury notes held in Social Security Trust Funds.

Current annual Social Security outlays are about $500 billion, or about 4 percent of GDP, and outlays will rise steadily as the baby-boom generation reaches retirement age. The official seventy-five-year actuarial projection forecasts that payroll taxes will continue to cover annual outlays until about 2019. From that point, tax collections will have to be supplemented by Trust Fund withdrawals, which will extend the system's solvency until about 2042. After the Trust Funds are exhausted, payroll tax collections will cover only about 70 percent of outlays. The total seventy-five-year deficit is equivalent to about 2 percent of the payroll tax—that is, an immediate tax increase to 14.4 percent of payrolls would restore the system to solvency without further changes.[3] But there are many other plausible reform alternatives; most of them include some mix of increases in the taxable payroll ceiling and tinkerings with benefit schedules, like modifying the "bend points" for upper-income retirees and changing cost-of-living formulas for retired recipients.[*]

---

* There is at least one set of proposals along these lines that has already been certified by the Social Security actuary. It should be noted that the Bush administration has publicized an actuarial imbalance calculated over an infinite forecast period primarily, it appears, for polemical effect. Even a seventy-five-year forecast enters the realm of vague hypothesis. Many analysts, moreover, regard the actuary's deficit forecast as unduly

Although the Social Security system will remain solvent for many years after the point where payroll taxes do not cover current outlays, drawing on the Trust Funds *will* have important implications for federal fiscal management. In most years since 1983, the federal government has balanced its budget by borrowing from (selling Treasury notes to) the Trust Funds. When the Trust Funds begin to draw upon their reserves, however, the cash flows will reverse and the government will have to raise cash to repay the accumulated notes. Continuation of the Bush administration's very large deficit spending patterns will therefore create serious future cash squeezes. Recent warnings from social conservatives, however, that the Trust Funds contain "no assets . . . [but] simply IOUs"[4] are irresponsible. They are legally issued Treasury securities, the most trusted financial instruments in the world, and their repudiation would have grave implications for world financial markets. (It is not obvious why conservatives should believe that private stocks and bonds are less risky—less of an "IOU"—than treasuries.)

MEDICARE AND MEDICAID

Medicare "Part A" provides insurance for hospital and related services for all Americans over sixty-five. It is financed by the proceeds of a 2.9 percent payroll tax (with no ceiling on covered earnings), which are paid into Trust Funds, like Social Security's. Outlays first exceeded payroll tax revenues in 2003, and the system has been balanced by drawing from general revenues since then. "Part B" for physician care is optional for Medicare-eligible Americans. Although it is nominally financed by beneficiary premiums, they currently cover only about a quarter of spending, with the rest made up from general tax revenues. Beginning in January 2006,

---

pessimistic. Economic growth rates assumed for the last fifty years of the forecast period are the lowest, by far, for any similarly extended period in American history. At normal historical growth rates, the projected deficit disappears. Surprisingly, the Bush privatization proposals assumed historical returns for private-market instruments, while using the actuary's very low economic forecast to project outcomes for the current system. Policymakers must have known that both could not be true.

there will be a new optional "Part D" providing partial coverage for prescription drugs, with a financing mechanism much like Part B's, although the details are still emerging.[5]

Medic*aid* is almost entirely a means-tested program financed from general revenues. It has important overlaps with the Medicare program, however, for it is the primary funder for long-term nursing home and home care for chronically ill people who have "spent down" their available resources. Except in limited circumstances, Medicare does not cover long-term care. Taken together, federal Medicare and Medicaid expenditures in fiscal year 2005/06 will nearly equal Social Security outlays, at just short of $500 billion, or another 4 percent of GDP, with Medicare accounting for about 60 percent of the total, not including state Medicaid matching spending of about $140 billion.[6] While Medicaid spending is theoretically easy to control through annual appropriations, recent extensions, like state programs to cover poor children, have become increasingly important as employers drop health insurance coverage for low-wage workers.

Over the longer term, absent major policy changes, Medicare is on course to be the largest federal expenditure program by far. Medicare outlays are forecast to exceed Social Security's by about 2024, and then to grow *much* larger. The federal deficit increment attributable to the administration's new "Part D" prescription drug program, by itself, is about twice the seventy-five-year Social Security deficit. The Medicare trustees currently forecast that Medicare alone will eventually consume 14 percent of GDP.[7]

THE SHAPE OF THE CRISIS II: PRIVATE SYSTEMS

PRIVATE SECTOR DEFINED BENEFIT PENSIONS

To the Depression-era generation entering the workforce after World War II, one of the secrets of the good life was to catch on with "a big company with a pension." Although fewer than half of private sector workers ever had a defined benefit pension,* it was one of the trademark features of the American dream—a defined benefit pension, promising a set monthly payment for the rest of your life, and usually your spouse's life, so long as you put in the service time. The first realization that pension promises were not ironclad may have come when the Studebaker Co. folded in 1963 and defaulted on its pension obligations. Congress eventually responded with the Employee Retirement Income Security Act (ERISA) of 1974. ERISA established financing and accounting standards for defined benefit pensions and created the federal Pension Benefit Guarantee Corporation (PBGC) to insure private defined benefit pension commitments.

The modern portfolio management industry is, to a great extent, a creature of ERISA's requirement that companies set aside assets to fund their future pension liabilities. If the actuarially determined present value of pension liabilities exceeds that of pension fund assets, the shortfall is subtracted from the company's net worth as if it were a debt. As of mid-2005, private companies have amassed $1.8 trillion in assets to support their defined benefit pension obligations, against future liabilities valued at about $2.2 trillion.[8] Pension funds initially concentrated their investments in high-grade bond portfolios, but as the stock market recovered through the 1980s, funds gradually shifted to higher-yielding stocks, in the hope that higher returns would allow reductions in annual contributions. During the 1990s market boom, stock returns were so high that many plans became overfunded, and pension funds actually became an important

---

* The percentage of employers offering plans was always substantially higher than employees covered, due to eligibility requirements. Female clerical workers in the 1950s, for example, tended to leave the workforce for childbearing before earning the service credits for coverage—although they were often covered by the spousal provisions in their husbands' plans. Welfare capitalism, that is, flourished alongside—and at a deep level assumed—the unusually stable family patterns of the postwar era.

driver of company earnings.* When the markets reversed after 2000, pension fund underperformance hammered profits, at the same time as falling operating earnings reduced companies' ability to increase plan contributions. Just as important, although not widely understood, the steady fall in interest rates after 2001 greatly ratcheted up the book value of future pension liabilities.**

The negative swing in corporate pension fund positions has been roughly $750 billion since 1999—from a $300 billion surplus to an estimated $450 billion deficit as of mid-2005. Analysts at CreditSuisse/First Boston (CSFB) recently published a list of twenty major companies with pension liabilities that equal or exceed the company's market value; the list includes Delta Airlines (which has since declared bankruptcy), with pension obligations 13 times higher than its market value; General Motors, 4.7 times higher; Ford, 2.7 times higher; Lucent, 1.9 times higher; and U.S. Steel, 1.4 times higher. Mounting deficits at the PBGC are creating the potential for a federal bailout on the scale of the 1980s Savings and Loan crisis. (Technically, the

---

* Pension fund performance affects earnings since changes in net liabilities flow through to the profit and loss statement. So over-target fund earnings (which reduce pension liabilities) will increase reported profits, while performance shortfalls reduce them. To prevent pension fund return fluctuations from dominating earnings reports, ERISA permits a variety of "smoothing" maneuvers, which create apparently irresistible opportunities for earnings manipulation.

** Falling interest rates reduce the "discount rate" used to value future pension liabilities. A lower discount rate makes a future liability *bigger*—and the effect can be very large. Press reports on the recent collapse of the United Airways pension plan tended to focus on the performance of its fund managers, which actually appears quite respectable. The real problem, along with a shortfall in United's contributions, was a big increase in the computed present value of its liabilities. Tax rules add further complications. To prevent the pension plan from being an all-weather tax shelter, the IRS disallows actuarially "excessive" contributions, which arguably prevents companies from shoring up plans in years when they are flush with cash. Legislation before the Congress would substantially loosen those rules, by rather more than Treasury officials believe prudent.

PBGC, which is supposed to be self-financing through fees and insurance premiums, has no legal call on the federal purse, but political pressure for a federal response could be overwhelming.)

A number of proposals are being floated to shore up defined benefit pension funding and accounting, but most would require companies to report higher levels of debt and lower profits. More likely, companies will accelerate the process of extracting themselves from their pension obligations. One path is the strategic bankruptcy. Shedding pension obligations has become practically a standardized financial engineering tool in the hands of private equity buyout managers—in steel companies, auto parts companies, and more recently, a string of airline bankrupcies. Collectively, it appears that United, Delta, and Northwestern airlines, and the auto parts maker Delphi will be relieved of some $32 billion in pension liabilities through the bankruptcy process. (The last four companies on that list have not yet officially requested a PBGC takeover, but that seems inevitable.[9]) Less dramatic alternatives include terminating a plan, or closing it to new employees, or converting it to a "cash balance" plan.[*10] Even financially healthy companies, like IBM, have been taking the cash balance route; at least a third of employees in nominally "defined benefit" pension plans have been converted to the cash balance format.

In short, the days when defined benefit pensions were a major support of American retirement systems are over.

---

* Plan termination is governed by a detailed set of ERISA rules to ensure that plan assets are equitably distributed to plan beneficiaries, although the details of particular distributions are often controversial. Cash balance plans pay the plan assets pro rata into individual accounts, usually with the promise of continued employer contributions. On retirement, the employee gets the contributions principal plus a modest (and easily hedgable) rate of interest. By definition, all unfunded liabilities disappear from the company's books. Long-term employees often lose significant benefits upon a conversion. Over the longer term, however, younger, more mobile employees—who are less likely to build sufficient defined benefit service credits—usually fare better under the cash balance option. Two of the most publicized recent cash balance conversions—IBM's and Xerox's—have been held up by age-discrimination lawsuits; cash balance plans themselves, however, are specifically permitted by ERISA.

Currently, only about 20 percent of private sector workers participate in defined benefit pensions,[11] and that number will drop to the vanishing point over the next ten years or so. Overall, defined benefit coverage is higher because almost all federal employees and up to 90 percent of state and local government employees are members of defined benefit plans. Analysts have estimated, however, that the unfunded liabilities of state and local defined benefit plans are even higher than in the private sector. Pension fund payments have become the fastest-growing items in many jurisdictions, squeezing out education and other essential spending. State issues of tens of billions of "pension obligation bonds" to take advantage of rising markets in the late 1990s have only worsened the problem.[12] The phasing in of private-sector-like accounting rules for state and local governments starting in the late 1990s is forcing accurate disclosure, although their initial effects have been masked by superb market returns—indeed, many jurisdictions fattened benefits. "Smoothing" provisions have also blunted the stated impact of market underperformance and falling discount rates, but the scale of the liability overhang cannot be suppressed much longer.[13]

PRIVATE SECTOR DEFINED CONTRIBUTION PENSIONS

Defined contribution pensions—primarily 401(k) plans—are employer-sponsored tax-advantaged savings and investment accounts under the control of the covered employee. Maximum contributions in any year are up to 20 percent of salary, not to exceed $14,000 at present. Labor Department survey data show that 53 percent of private sector employees had access to a defined contribution plan in 2004, and 42 percent actually participated in a plan. In about 80 percent of the defined contribution plans, the employer makes some form of a matching contribution. Total defined contribution pension assets in mid-2005, at some $2.7 trillion, are about 50 percent greater than defined benefit plan assets.[14]

A major advantage of defined contribution plans is that, unlike defined benefit pensions, they are portable—when an employee leaves a firm, the defined contribution account goes with her. Vesting rules usually apply to the employer's contribution, although they are typically more lenient than those for defined benefit plans. During the initial proliferation of defined contribution plans, they were often badly abused by employers— by requiring employees to invest their accounts in the sponsoring company stock, for example. Current rules have eliminated the worst abuses and ensure that employees are offered a reasonable menu of investment alternatives. Companies are realizing as well that most employees need advice on basic investment strategies: left to their own devices, many merely concentrate their funds in cash-like accounts, foregoing the opportunities for compounded returns.

The primary problem with defined contribution pensions— even leaving aside the more than half of all private sector workers who have *neither* a defined benefit or a defined contribution plan—is the paltriness of the coverage built up by the average worker. A Census Bureau survey of household asset holdings in 2000 showed that the middle-quintile income household, with a middle-aged household head (45–54), had net financial assets of just $12,725, plus $43,917 of home equity. Among all middle-quintile households, only a quarter held any 401(k) or other thrift-type asset, fewer than 20 percent had IRAs or similar instruments (in the lowest quintile, fewer than 9 percent), and even fewer held any stocks or mutual funds other than those in their retirement accounts. Earners in the two lower quintiles, for all practical purposes, had almost no retirement savings at all.[15]

A study by the Congressional Budget Office teased out participation rates in tax-advantaged programs from 1997 tax returns. The study uses different income categories from the Census Bureau's and, because of the nature of the data, did not break out private sector employees. Among all income groups, however, only 27 percent participated in 401(k) or similar plans. Participation among the low earners was only 6 percent, rising to more than 50 percent in households earning more than $80,000. Not surprisingly, only 1 percent of the low-earning households with 401(k)s made any contributions

FIGURE 3.3. CONSEQUENCES OF AN EMPLOYER-BASED SYSTEM

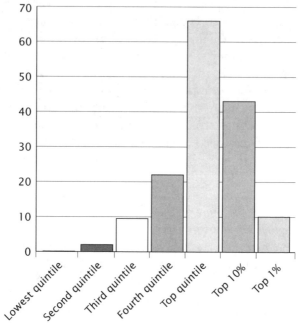

Source: Peter Orszag and Robert Greenstein, "Toward Progressive Pensions: A Summary of the U.S. Pension System and Proposals for Reform," Pension Rights Center (2001), p. 10.

in the year surveyed; but strikingly, in households earning between $40,000 and $80,000, only 4 percent made the maximum contribution. Even worse, one recent survey showed that 45 percent of workers—and 42 percent of workers aged 40–49—withdrew all their plan contributions when they changed jobs.[16] The rate of participation in IRAs and other nonemployment-based savings programs is even lower: a risible 6 percent of all earners—2 percent in the low-earning households and 17 percent among the top earners (above $160,000). Total IRA assets, however, at $3.4 trillion are nearly triple the assets in defined benefit pension funds and about a quarter larger than defined contribution pension assets.[17] Ownership of those assets obviously is skewed toward the upper-income quintiles (see Figure 3.3).

Further, the data make clear that attempts to increase savings by raising the ceilings on devices like IRAs and 401(k)s is about the *least* efficient method that could be chosen, although it is the favorite resort of the Bush administration and the Congress. Based on 1999 tax returns, the Treasury Department estimated that about two-thirds of the value of the tax deductions for IRA and defined contribution pension contributions accrued to top quintile earners, with a strong skew toward the richest of the rich earners—43 percent of the tax deductions went to the top 10 percent of earners, while a full tenth of the deductions went to just the top 1 percent of earners.[18] Much of the apparent increment in upper-income savings, moreover, is really fund-shifting from taxable to tax-advantaged accounts. Raising ceilings on tax-based savings instruments, in short, is just a backdoor way to shower even more tax cuts on the well-to-do. Absurdly, the annual federal revenue foregone by tax-based savings incentives now exceeds annual household savings.[19]

In the final analysis, however, the retirement finance problem is probably not nearly as serious as the health care financing challenge. Some academic economists, indeed, suspect that the retirement savings issue is being exaggerated by the fund management industry. One study, for example, based on results from a representative panel of people born between 1931 and 1941, finds that 80 percent of the panel had either adequate savings, or more than they needed. Average shortfalls of the undersavers, moreover, were not large. A key point was that for the poorest third of the cohort, who generally had little or no savings, Social Security income was sufficient for their needs—which is consistent with the low rate of poverty among the elderly, and a long-term trend toward earlier retirement.[20] An important concern is whether the recent collapse in household savings (see Chapter 4), especially if it is accompanied by a flattening or downturn in house prices, will generate significantly different outcomes for the next cohorts of retirees. This is clearly an area where there is a pressing need for continued, empirical, policy-related research.

FIGURE 3.4. THE FLIGHT FROM BENEFIT PROVISION

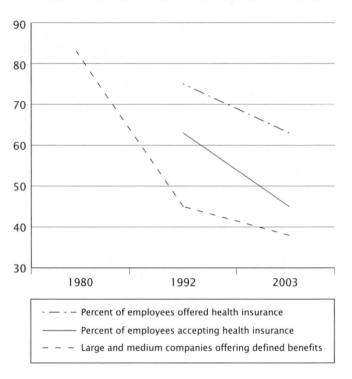

Source: William J. Waitrowski, "Comparing Employee Benefits in the Public and Private Sector," *Monthly Labor Review,* December 1988, pp. 3–8; William J. Waitrowski, "Medical and Retirement Plan Coverage: Explaining the Decline in Recent Years," *Monthly Labor Review,* August 2004, pp. 29–36.

PRIVATE HEALTH INSURANCE COVERAGE

According to the Census Bureau, some 15.7 percent of non-elderly Americans, or 45.8 million people, had no health insurance coverage in 2004. The percentage of the uncovered non-elderly has been rising slowly, with some ups and downs, from 12.9 percent in 1987 when the data were first collected. The peak figure was 16.3 percent in 1998; the number fell to 14.2 percent in 2000, presumably as a consequence of the late-1990s boom, before it began increasing again (see Figure 3.4).

The 45.8 million figure, it should be noted, is from an annual *point-in-time* sample. The number of individuals without health coverage at any time during 2004 was in the range of 69 million, while the number without coverage for the entire year was about 30 million. Some portion of the uninsured, moreover, are clearly not hardship cases. A surprising 8.4 percent of people with incomes over $75,000 did not have health insurance in 2004, while 31.4 percent of 18–24-year-olds were uncovered. Many younger people doubtless did not bother, or regarded their parents' credit cards as sufficient insurance in an emergency.[21]

At the same time, raw data on the percentages of uncovered do not fully capture the growing hardship. Since 2001, the cost of employer-based health care insurance has increased by 2.5 times the rate of inflation, much faster than any other compensation cost.[22] Employers have responded either by dropping health care benefits entirely, or by pushing more of the costs onto their employees. The trend has been particularly harsh in smaller businesses, in nonunionized shops, and in businesses paying the lowest wages. Small businesses also were far more likely to require employee contributions and generally had the lowest rates of eligible employee sign ups. Since 1999 the percentage of all private sector employees required to contribute to single-coverage insurance has risen from two-thirds to three-quarters, while contributions for family coverage are now nearly universal.[23] A mid-2005 survey by the Kaiser Family Foundation found that the average family coverage plan cost $906/month, and the median employee contribution was $226/month.[24] Since the average cost of family coverage is now slightly more than the U.S. minimum wage, it is out of the reach of most low-wage employees and probably their employers.

The net result is that many families are choosing to go without insurance. Fully 45 percent of the uninsured in 2004, or 21 million people in the point sample, were in households where at least one person worked full-time for the year. The great majority of the uninsured—70 percent according to a Kaiser Family Foundation survey—are uninsured because they cannot afford coverage, and are consciously forgoing health care that they believe they need.[25] Hospital clinics, of course, dispense a lot of charity care. But a study of automobile accident victims, a relatively pure case where initial decisions are in control of the receiving hospital, found real treatment differences between the insured and uninsured, and the lower levels of treatment for the uninsured were associated with higher death rates.[26] Heavy uninsured medical expenses are one of the leading causes of personal bankruptcy.

Employers also are straining under the pressure, even at very large, new-economy companies. Starbucks employs 100,000 people, the majority of them part-time, and provides health insurance to everyone working more than a twenty-hour week. Its founder and chairman, Howard Schultz, recently noted that the company now spends more on health insurance than on purchasing coffee, which he called "unsustainable."[27] William Clay Ford, chairman of the Ford Motor Co., told a business group in 2004 that "During the four-year period through 2003, [Ford's] health insurance premiums increased by 11.4 percent a year, compared to 2.2 percent for overall inflation. This is a pace we cannot sustain. . . . I am suggesting using all of the efficiencies of the market, along with the proper role of the government to provide better health care at a better price." While Ford suggested using the Medicare prescription drug program as a model for a solution, he hastened to add: "I want to make it clear that we are in no way suggesting a slow march to national health care."[28] Of course not.

Conservative leaders, and Mr. Ford, may deplore a "slow march to national health care," but it is happening anyway. By the end of the year, government agencies were paying for about 46 percent of American health care, most of it from general tax revenues. President Bush's prescription drug program will doubtless kick the government share over the 50 percent mark. The percentage of Americans without health insurance was unchanged between 2003 and 2004, but that was only because increased coverage under military programs and expansions in Medicaid, like the SCHIP (State Children's Health Insurance Program) coverage for poor children, masked the continued erosion of private insurance. The percentage of Americans covered by employer-sponsored plans fell to only 59.8 percent in 2004.[*29]

---

* Down from a recent peak of 64.1 percent in 2000. In the early 1990s recession, employment-based coverage fell even lower, to only 57.1 percent

Summary

All four of the basic pillars of the American social insurance system are in serious difficulty: despite its well-publicized problems, Social Security is arguably in the best shape of all. The promise of "golden-age" welfare capitalism to see to the retirement income and health care needs of its workers has clearly broken down. There are serious questions about whether American workers are acquiring adequate resources for retirement, and the day is approaching when only a minority of employers will offer health insurance at all. And these problems are all on the cusp of becoming *much* worse as the baby-boom generation becomes a massive consumer of retirement and health care resources.

Before addressing the requirements of adequate reform plans, however, the next two chapters will look briefly at critical trends in American incomes and saving patterns and at special features of the American health care system that provide an essential context for evaluating alternatives.

---

in 1993. But the fall in coverage was related to the high unemployment rate (7.4 percent in January 1993). When employment recovered strongly in 1994 and 1995 (dropping to 5.6 percent by the end of 1995), employment-based health coverage increased four percentage points to 61.1 percent. The recent declines, however, have occurred during a time of generally low unemployment rates (only 5.4 percent by year-end 2004), and are more likely caused by the growing percentage of employers who either do not offer coverage or who require high employee contributions. Although different surveys produce slightly different numbers, they show the same trends. Another recent federal survey found that availability of health insurance coverage in the private sector *rose* from 1996 to 2002 to 88.3 percent, a much higher percentage than in the Labor Department surveys, but that *eligibility* for health insurance went down, and *participation* fell even faster, so only 62.4 percent of employees were enrolled. The most important reason for declining participation, according to the study, was steady increases in required employee contributions.

4

RECENT TRENDS IN INCOME, DEBT, AND WEALTH IN THE UNITED STATES

The sharp pullback in employer-based benefit programs, and heightened worries about the stability of government-sponsored retirement and health insurance, could hardly come at a less auspicious time. For almost the past quarter-century, middle-income family budgets have been under unusual pressure. Figure 4.1 (page 32) captures some of the important trends in household incomes and worker earnings between 1980 and 2004.

The first two bars on Figure 4.1 show that, while both median and mean household money incomes have grown over the past quarter-century, mean household incomes have grown about twice as fast as median incomes—1.2 percent a year, on average, compared to 0.6 percent. (The *median* is the midpoint of a sample, while the *mean* is the arithmetic average. Changes in the numbers on either end of a distribution will affect the mean, but not the median.) The increasing spread between the mean and the median household incomes reflects the relatively bigger income gains for upper-bracket earners—while middle-income earners were treading water, there was a major stretching-out of

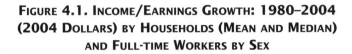

FIGURE 4.1. INCOME/EARNINGS GROWTH: 1980–2004 (2004 DOLLARS) BY HOUSEHOLDS (MEAN AND MEDIAN) AND FULL-TIME WORKERS BY SEX

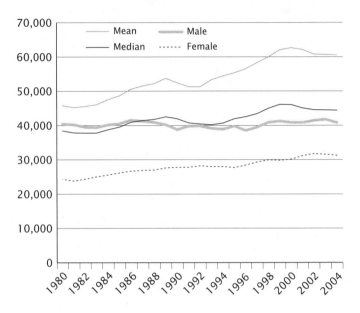

Source: Census Bureau, "Income, Poverty, and Health Insurance Coverage in the United States: 2004," Tables A-1, A-2.

the income range for the top half. The widening gap between the median and the mean has been a consistent pattern over the entire period. Even when both median and mean incomes fell between 1989 and 1993, for example, the median fell faster. The modest improvement in median household incomes, moreover, is entirely related to increased income for women. The earnings of full-time male workers have been flat over the entire period—$40,412 in 1980 (in 2004 dollars) and $40,798 in 2004. Females did much better: their median earnings rose from $24,312 in 1980 to $31,223 in 2004.[1]

Figure 4.2 illustrates the rewards gap between top-quintile households and the rest of the workforce. The period since 1980 represents the first time since the Great Depression that

FIGURE 4.2. MEDIAN INCOME GAINS BY QUINTILE: HOUSEHOLDS, 1980–2004 (2004 DOLLARS)

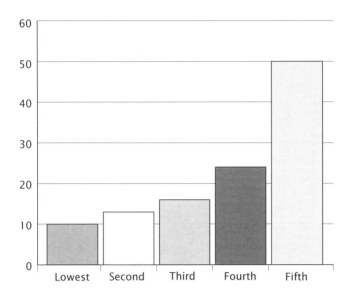

Source: Census Bureau, "Income, Poverty, and Health Insurance Coverage in the United States: 2004," Calculated by author from Table A-3.

improvements in household incomes did not move more or less in lockstep—lower-income households, that is, had usually seen their incomes grow at about the same percentage rate as upper-income households. Since 1980, the top brackets have done the best, and the percentage gains are smaller as households get poorer.

Conservative economists point out, quite correctly, that the Census Bureau's data conventions tend to overstate the advantage of the upper quintiles. Census income data are collected by *households,* not individuals, and the number of individuals in upper-income households has been growing faster than in lower-income households—so while each quintile contains 20 percent of the households, the top quintile has 30 percent of the people and the bottom quintile has only 14 percent. If the quintiles are rearranged so they each contain the same number of people, the top quintile's

FIGURE **4.3.** EARNINGS SHARE GAINS, TOP 10 PERCENT OF
EARNERS: 1980–2002 (2002 DOLLARS)

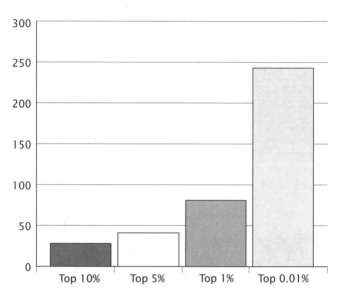

Source: Emmanuel Saez and Wojciech Kopzuk, "Top Wealth Shares in the
United States," *NBER Working Paper 10339,* March 2004, Figures 1–4.

advantage over the bottom drops from about 14 to 1 to about 10 to
1, which is still quite substantial. The differences narrow even more
if the earnings figures are adjusted to include government transfers
to the poor, and the longer hours that richer people work. But those
also are indications of reduced opportunity for the less skilled; the
history of welfare-reform work experience programs suggests that
only a minority of the poor remain unemployed by choice.[2]

But the truly dramatic income shift of the last couple decades
is not the increased advantage of rich versus poor, but the amaz-
ing concentration of income within the narrow coterie of the
superrich, to an extent not seen since 1929 (not an especially auspicious date). Economists have reanalyzed the Census data
through 2002 to break out relative share changes within the top
10 percent. (In Figure 4.3, the right-most bar represents the top
one-hundredth of 1 percent of households.)

FIGURE 4.4. INFLATION-ADJUSTED INCOME GAINS BY QUINTILE, 2002–2003, WITH DETAIL FOR TOP QUINTILE

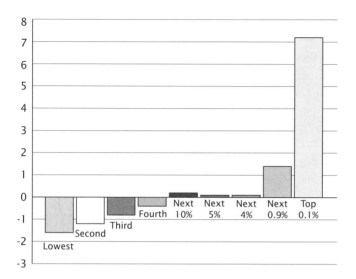

Source: Internal Revenue Service/*New York Times,* October 5, 2005 (Inflation for the period was 2.3 percent).

That trend is not slowing. Taxpayer data—which match the Census household category closely, but not exactly—reinforce the extent of the recent skewing of income gains. Figure 4.4 shows earners' quintile changes for the year 2003, the first year in which the full impact of the Bush tax cuts would have been felt. Concerns over the nuances of quintile groupings cease to be important, since the *entire bottom 99 percent* of earners lost ground to inflation in 2003, while the top 1 percent, and especially the top tenth of 1 percent of earners did very well indeed. The top tenth of 1 percent of earners, in fact, captured a fourth of all income gains. And the IRS notes that reporting protocols for higher-income households may understate the real gains at the top. (Note that the tax data cannot be analyzed down to the top one-hundredth of 1 percent [.01 percent] of earners as in the previous figure; otherwise, the maldistribution would appear even worse.)

The sudden shift in the pattern of income distribution is doubtless the consequence of the prolonged financial market boom that got under way in the mid-1980s, bringing in its wake wretched excesses not seen since the Gilded Age. In 1970, the top tenth of the top 10 percent of earners (or the top 0.01 percent of all earners) made, on average, about 17 times as much as the "typical" top-10 percent earner. By 2000, mostly because of an explosion in top management pay, that gap had jumped to 75 *times* as much—although it narrowed a bit, to only 55 times as much, during the 2001 recession. People making a mere $100,000 a year, perhaps, should feel aggrieved.[3] The Bush administration's tax cut program, however, instead of braking the skew toward the very wealthy, seems designed to accelerate it. Almost half of all the tax cuts accrue to the wealthiest 5 percent of households, and the proportionate income gains to the wealthiest 1 percent of households are triple those for middle-income households.[4] Rubbing it in, the administration makes no secret that the enormous loss in federal revenue will be made up partly by cutting programs that benefit the lower quintiles.

YET . . . STILL A CONSUMER BOOM

Despite the lagging income growth for the average middle-income household, consumers still have managed to be the main engine of the economy over most of the period. But they did it by running down their savings and sharply increasing their debt burdens. Personal savings dropped from 10 percent of disposable income in 1980 to only 1.8 percent in 2004. For the entire quarter ending in August 2005, personal savings were essentially zero (0.1 percent of income), the lowest savings level since the data series was created. But over the twelve months to August 2005, consumer spending grew by a robust 4 percent over inflation—or about two-thirds faster than the growth in income. Personal debt in the meanwhile ballooned to historically high levels, to 119 percent of disposable income in 2004, up from only 70 percent in 1980. About 70 percent of consumer debt is borrowed against houses, and most of the rest is consumer credit, much of it at crushing interest rates.

Superficially, the increase in the net worth of American households since 2000 looks fairly strong—up by $6.8 trillion through the first quarter of 2005—but half of that increase was due to the increase in the net market value of housing.* The growth in the market value of household real estate (51.6 percent), moreover, was outpaced by the growth in mortgages outstanding (up by 60.5 percent).[5] And in recent years, more and more of mortgage finance has been to maintain household liquidity. The housing finance agency, Freddie Mac, estimates that home refinancing will generate $162 billion of household cash flow in 2005, or substantially more than estimated 2005 personal savings.[6] The market value of American homes now accounts for about a third of all personal assets, the highest level ever. Merrill Lynch estimates that about half of all American GDP growth in the first half of 2005 was housing-related, either directly through home-building and purchasing, or indirectly, by spending refinancing cash flows; more than half of all new private-sector jobs since 2001, it calculates, were in housing-related activities.[7]

A prolonged period of low interest rates, in short, and an unusually permissive banking regulatory regime, has led to a huge consumer debt overhang, much of it of very poor quality. According to the FDIC, sub-prime lending accounted for about 20 percent of mortgage financings in 2004, while 46 percent of financings were floating-rate or other nonstandard loans designed to minimize initial-period cash outflows.[8] Much of that borrowing, moreover, has gone to pay down very expensive credit card lines.[9] And there are abundant signs of a potential slowdown or downturn in home prices. New housing starts are far outrunning the rate of new household formation, while housing affordability indices, which relate home prices to household incomes, are

---

* Almost all the rest was in just two categories—household stock-holdings and shares in unincorporated businesses, like stock brokerages. Both of those are concentrated in top earning households, leaving home price appreciation as the primary, almost the sole, source of wealth accumulation among the rest of the population.

among the worst ever.[10] Even a relatively modest reversal in home prices plus a rate-driven increase in mortgage debt service will leave consumers painfully exposed.

Finally, it is not obvious that the heavy borrowing and the collapse of savings are driven mostly by feckless consumption. In their book, *The Two-Income Trap: Why Middle-Class Parents Are Going Broke,* Elizabeth Warren and Amelia Tyagi argue that the typical two-earner middle-income family has *less* disposable income after deducting for reasonable necessities than its one-earner counterpart thirty years ago, especially if it has children.[11] (Their data are based in part on the Consumer Bankruptcy Project, a large database of bankrupt families maintained at the Harvard Business School.) The house-price premium for a good school district, for example, is beginning to approach the scale of private school tuition, while the spread-out design of modern suburbs necessitates second cars and cell phones to stay in touch. A bankruptcy database shows that the primary causes of household bankruptcies are loss of a job, a divorce, and heavy medical expenses in that order, not luxury consumption, and that it is the middle-class families who are most likely to file for protection. Statistically, a two-earner family is more apt to lose a job than a single-earner family, and since the typical family now has little financial cushion, it is only a short step from a temporary reduction in income to a tangle of credit-card cash advances at ruinous interest rates.

In short, the economic environment for building a comfortable national savings surplus to ensure reasonable retirement prospects and to finance an expanding health care sector could hardly be less auspicious.

5

THE SPECIAL CASE OF HEALTH CARE

Almost no one disagrees that the American health care system is badly in need of thoroughgoing reform and reengineering. Yet the very noisy current debate over the future of American health care rarely comes to grips with the intrinsic features of health care in general, and of the American health care system in particular, that must be taken into account for reform to be successful.

This chapter will attempt to set out certain special characteristics of health care, some positive and some negative, that consistently defeat initiatives of both liberal and conservative provenance to "bring health care spending under control."

On the positive side, the tendency of health care to consume an ever-larger share of GDP is perfectly consistent with the long-term shift of resources, in all wealthy countries, toward services and away from food production and basic manufacturing. The health care industry in particular offers very attractive features as a technology driver, and as a positive contributor to employment growth, productivity, and the trade balance. The widespread assumption that we would be better off if we *reduced* health care's share of GDP is simply wrong.

On the negative side, there are features of American health care, mostly derived from its roots in welfare capitalism, that make it unusually expensive compared to other national systems. Further, considered purely as an operational system, health care is a mess. The artisanal, solo/small-group practice model of delivering health care traditionally favored by the medical profession has utterly failed to keep pace either with medical technology, or with the evolving service needs posed by wealthy-country demographics.

Finally, a realistic view of consumer and provider decision-making behavior suggests that the consumer-market reform models so favored by political conservatives are not only inadequate, and largely irrelevant, to the reform challenge, but also are likely to cause even greater waste of resources. Those special features of health care are briefly expanded upon in the rest of this chapter.

1. THE STEADY EXPANSION OF HEALTH CARE'S SHARE OF GDP IS DRIVEN BY DEEP ECONOMIC FORCES, AND WILL CONTINUE FOR THE FORESEEABLE FUTURE.

One hundred and fifty years ago, about 60 percent of American workers were employed in agriculture and families spent 50 percent of their income on food; today, agriculture employs about 2 percent of the workforce, while only about 14 percent of the consumer budget goes to food (including restaurant meals), although most Americans have far too much to eat. Fifty years ago, about 33 percent of all American workers were employed in manufacturing; today, only 10 percent are, but the inflation-adjusted value of their output is far higher.* The United States is still the world leader in real manufacturing output, and far ahead of China, which has six times as many manufacturing workers.[1] In short, large shifts in spending and employment patterns are both normal and reflect underlying productivity gains. There also are fundamental reasons why health care's expansion should outrun most other services. As nations get richer, the marginal value of

---

* In this case, inflation-adjustment is to account for the dramatic fall in the price of most manufactured goods, along with large increases in their functionality.

FIGURE 5.1. "SQUEEZING OUT" BY HEALTH CARE IS GROSSLY OVERSTATED

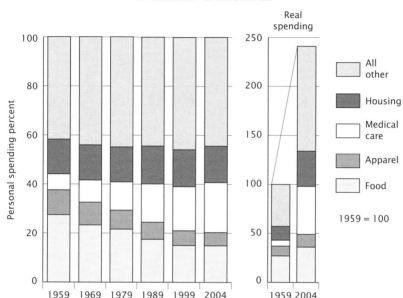

Source: Author's calculations from Bureau of Economic Analysis National Income and Product Accounts, August 2005, and the Bureau of Labor Statistics Consumer Price Index.

increased consumption (that is, the extra enjoyment from one more toy) falls below the marginal value of a longer life (to enjoy all of one's toys). One recent paper, based on such shifting calculations, estimates that health care spending should rise to about a third of GDP, or twice its current share.[2]

Further, it is not true that health care spending has been squeezing out other necessities (see Figure 5.1). Americans now spend somewhat *less* of their disposable incomes on "essentials"—food, clothing, housing, and health care—than they did fifty years ago. (Spending on food and clothing is a far smaller fraction of income; housing's spending share has been roughly flat, although homes are much bigger and better-appointed; while health care's spending share has risen sharply.[3]) Since incomes have grown strongly over that same period, the income available for spending on everything else has risen strongly as well. Finally, even at relatively low levels of economic growth, the share of health care in GDP can expand for a very long time before it begins to crowd out anything at all. The continued trend line toward more health care and other services is fully in accord with historical experience.

2. HEALTH CARE IS A WEALTH-CREATING, HIGH TECHNOLOGY, RELATIVELY HIGH-PRODUCTIVITY INDUSTRY.

It was once an economic truism that service industries were generally not susceptible to productivity increases. (How to improve the productivity of a string quartet, or a kindergarten teacher?) In recent decades, however, high technology has transformed the productivity of most service industries—in financial services, for example, substituting computers for people has made the industry a national productivity leader. Health care productivity growth, while not as startling as in financial services, is still well above average and accelerating.[4]

Health care makes up about 15 percent of American stock market capitalization—roughly its share of GDP—and the industry is generally a good employer that pays above-average wages. The very high technology component in modern health care is an important source of semiprofessional, technician-level employment (as imaging technicians, perfusionists, dental hygienists, inhalation therapists, and many, many others). Companies like General Electric HealthCare (imaging, diagnostics, pharmaceutical manufacturing systems, patient monitoring systems, 43,000 employees, $15 billion in sales) are world leaders. Health care is an important driver of advances in electronics and biotechnology, is not especially susceptible to outsourcing, and is a positive contributor to the American current account balance.

Procedure by procedure, moreover, technological advances have generally *reduced* costs, often by quite striking amounts, while bringing very large benefits in terms of extended, active life spans. The very sharp drop in the death rate from heart attacks, for example, is substantially attributable to improvements in the technology of cardiac interventions. Modern pharmaceuticals are making major inroads in the treatment of depression, hypertension, diabetes, arthritis, and other chronic diseases, as well as steady advances against cancer. Surgical interventions to remove cataracts, to replace hips, knees, and even eye and ear parts, keep people active longer, while laparoscopic and other microsurgical techniques make interventions quicker and safer, and greatly improve recovery times, and MRIs replace older invasive, often dangerous, diagnostic procedures.

The sudden accession of less expensive and more effective health care technologies, however, just as in personal computers and consumer electronics, has greatly expanded the health care market and consequently increased *spending*. Most gall bladder surgery, for example, is now performed on an outpatient basis: it is cheaper, requires minimal incisions, and gets you back to work sooner. So doctors are more apt to recommend it, and total outlays keep rising. The same is true of a long list of other standard procedures—cataract surgery is now a simple outpatient procedure that costs a fraction of what it used to, so millions of Americans have had it. Hip operations are surer and safer, with rapidly improving recovery times, so they are almost a rite of passage for senior golfers. The same is true of thrombolytic stents, fast bedside test kits, and a whole range of interventions to help premature babies, who previously would have died or been seriously disabled, recover to a normal development path. It is not falling productivity that is driving costs, that is, but the expanding basket of effective interventions—both for diseases doctors have always treated, and for a growing list of conditions previously beyond our reach.[5]

3. THERE ARE FEATURES OF AMERICAN HEALTH CARE, ROOTED IN ITS WELFARE CAPITALIST ORIGINS, THAT LEAD TO UNUSUALLY HIGH COSTS COMPARED TO OTHER NATIONAL SYSTEMS.

Welfare capitalism's benefit systems, at bottom, were designed to serve the interests of the firm, and so are tilted to support business recruitment and retention objectives. Core benefit programs typically have a pronounced skew toward the higher-pay, white-collar and professional employee ranks. In health care, that inherent bias has left a deep stamp on the internal workings of the industry.

A fair listing of the core values of American health care would include: a deep commitment to a high rate of technological innovation; a penchant for rich and complex service arrays; a devotion to consumer choice; and a notable willingness to allow patients to shop among specialists and treatment options. In practice, those values have translated into extraordinary accomplishments in cutting-edge medicine; a free-wheeling, laissez-faire approach to the introduction of new, often unproven, technologies; hit-or-miss coordination of services; and very high costs. In short, it is nearly an ideal system for the affluent, educated professionals with comprehensive benefit packages. But for the less well-off and less well-educated, the system is confusing, burdensomely expensive, and occasionally dangerous, if it is accessible at all.

Making the system simpler and more uniform inevitably means limiting choices. But legislators typically recoil from the notion of permissible care baskets,* or dollar caps for treatments.[6] (It is ironic, in a nation that so celebrates the privileges of wealth, that politicians tend to insist that everyone deserves the same level of health care as the very rich.) An aggressive program to rein in prescription drug costs in Oregon, for example, was approved

---

* The "Oregon Plan," an expanded Medicaid program for the uninsured who do not meet federal eligibility standards, is a rare instance of explicit care rationing. A state commission assigns a priority rating to a comprehensive list of "condition/treatment" pairs, through a mixture of cost-effectiveness data and public hearings. As part of the annual budgeting process "a line is drawn" after the lowest-ranking covered priority, and anything that misses the cut is excluded. A scholarly analysis of actual practice, however, found that the excluded items were much like those in conventional insurance plans, and were somewhat more generous than in the previous Medicaid regime. Items like organ transplants (highly expensive with few beneficiaries) that had figured prominently in the legislative debates are in fact mostly included, and actual savings have been small. The plan has still been an important milestone for the principle of rationalized care allocation.

by the legislature on the condition that there be no limitation on drugs for cancer or HIV-AIDS, and the legislature subsequently prohibited the administration from establishing a prior-approval process for drugs not on an approved list—in effect, reducing the program to an educational campaign. New York state legislators repeatedly have blocked initiatives to impose even minimal controls on Medicaid drug spending. The same legislators undoubtedly fume about "rising health care costs" during annual budget cycles.[7]

Wonkish hopes that "evidence-based" medicine and cost-effectiveness studies can provide politically neutral decision tools are likely to be disappointed. Advocates for evidence-based medicine, for example, often sound as if their discipline ferrets out only instances of *over*treatment, ignoring the wide swathes of health care where people are likely to be *under*treated—probably twice as many people should be taking asthma drugs as currently, and ten times as many should be on anticholesterol drugs.[8] Subjecting each new therapy or technology—much less each *old* therapy—to a full-blown evidence-based analysis would be astronomically expensive. And even the paradigmatic demonstrations of savings from evidence-based principles apply only at a micro-level. If maintaining an aspirin regimen obviates a cardiac bypass, that is clearly a gain for the patient *at that time*. But if the patient lives longer as a consequence, he will go on consuming health care resources, and may sooner or later have the bypass operation anyway.

The iron logic of health care is that the longer people live, the more they cost. The economist's "cost-benefit" for each death prevented—usually $100,000—is priced in metaphysical dollars that appear on nobody's income statement. Reducing smoking extends life spans *and* increases health care costs. Grandma's extra years of life may boost her family's happiness quotient, but do not help pay off the federal debt.[9] Evidence-based and cost-effectiveness decision tools may help prevent spending *foolishly*, but there is no reason to believe that they will lead to spending less.

The ceaseless lobbying by provider interest groups makes an inherently difficult problem much worse. Pharmaceutical companies and equipment manufacturers, chiropractors and chiropodists, lay siege to state and federal legislators to remove limitations on their coverage, to raise reimbursement rates, or to anoint their products as "basic services." The pervasiveness of consulting agreements and other subterfuges that direct income to doctors who tout particular brands of gear or pills is a continuing scandal. Market-oriented conservatives, oddly, raised little din when an allegedly conservative Congress and administration forbade Medicare staff *by law* from negotiating pharmaceutical prices under the new Medicare drug plan.

4. OPERATIONALLY, AMERICAN HEALTH CARE IS A DISGRACE, IN
GREAT PART BECAUSE OF A FUNDAMENTAL MISMATCH BETWEEN
SERVICE CONTENT AND THE DELIVERY SYSTEM.

If the same degree of quality control seen in modern medicine were applied in making computers or cars, companies would have been out of business long ago. Studies have shown, for example, that the confidence of a doctor in a diagnosis is only "weakly" correlated with the accuracy of the diagnosis, and that a great many physicians either are not familiar with, do not agree with, or do not follow, currently accepted best practices in their specialties. The handoff of a patient from one care-stage to another is often utterly unmanaged. A depressingly high percentage of hospital discharge test results, for example, either never get to, or are never read by, the treating physician. Most physicians admit to little or no interest in quality assurance techniques, and only about a third have access to quality information either on their own practices or on the specialists to whom they refer patients.[10]

Although the FDA does reasonably rigorous testing on the safety and effectiveness of new pharmaceuticals, there is little systematic followup on their longer-term effects, nor typically, comparisons of effectiveness with cheaper, off-patent drugs. Once a drug is approved, moreover, physicians are free to prescribe it for any disease at all, not just the ones it has been tested for. The obstacles to introducing new medical devices or new surgical procedures are even more porous, ranging from the very modest to none at all. Minimally invasive surgical techniques are a wonderful improvement, but they are tricky and carry special dangers. Their wildfire-spread through the surgical community in the early 1990s, before techniques or tools had been at all standardized, must have placed many patients at risk.[11]

The continuing proliferation of promising new health care interventions, moreover, makes the quality control challenge ever more pressing. The very high survival rate among heart attack victims, for example, means that several million people *who have had* heart attacks not only need continuing medical care, but also will survive to contract other diseases of aging, like cancers, renal disease, diabetes, arthritis, and cognitive disorders. A relatively small percentage of patients with two or more such diseases account for the vast majority of Medicare spending; the 20 percent of Medicare patients with five or more chronic conditions have, on average, *fourteen different* physicians.[12] Yet the standard Medicare fee-for-service program offers "[f]ew incentives and less infra-structure" for chronic disease management or treatment coordination.[13] In effect, it is up to the patient, often a very ill and confused patient, to keep all her doctors informed about what is going on, to track medications accurately, and to see that the right providers are kept current on critical tests and recent diagnoses.

The quality and coordination problems are not even close to being addressed. Most doctors still work in an essentially 1950s-vintage, solo or small-group practice mode, one that was well adapted to low-technology medicine targeted at a generally young patient population. Even now, most of individuals' contacts with doctors—for checkups, treatment of minor infections, injuries, preventive testing, minor surgery, and the like—probably are quite adequately handled within the traditional organization, but they account for only a minor portion of the health care budget. Some 80 percent of all health care resources are consumed by the seriously ill—the 10–20 percent of patients who suffer from multiple, major diseases. Taking care of those patients poses a management challenge that the artisanal practice model is almost perversely ill-equipped to deal with.

Businesses that pursue Six Sigma or Total Quality Management programs in complex manufacturing or service environments maintain obsessive vigilance over defects, build systems to pin them on offending processes or managers, and create expert "SWAT" teams to redesign offending operations

or replace underperforming managers. Health care can indeed
boast of local single-disease silos of excellence, as in heart disease
or cancer; but by a modern business standard, the industry is
disgracefully unmanaged and devoid of meaningful quality systems. Tellingly, the predominant bias is to *suppress* evidence of
failures because of the threat of malpractice suits.

Treating patients is not like making computer chips, for no
patient's bio-reactions are precisely like any other's. But for most
diseases, or presenting symptoms, there are well-established diagnostic and treatment protocols to channel an analysis in the most
promising directions, and the data suggest they are honored
mostly in the breach. A few organizations, like the Kaiser
Permanente groups, have imposed medical management layers
over their in-house physicians and made measurable improvements in quality. It was Kaiser's tracking systems that first flagged
the problems with Vioxx, for example, and they generally have
excellent rates of compliance in, say, prescribing beta-blockers
for cardiac patients (which significantly reduces the risk of a second attack). But the Kaiser plans are exceptional; most HMOs are
just billing and payment machines. Aside from very simple monitoring, like flagging potentially dangerous drug interactions, they
mostly leave their physicians alone. And even the Kaiser systems
are rudimentary by Six Sigma standards.

Unfortunately, there are few grounds for expecting major
progress in fixing health care's operational tangle. Creating management systems equal to a fast-moving, high-technology enterprise
like modern medicine would be a formidable challenge under the
best of circumstances, but it may be hopeless so long as physician
independence remains the touchstone of the industry's organization.

5. THE "MARKET-ORIENTED" HEALTH CARE REFORMS CURRENTLY
PUSHED BY MARKET CONSERVATIVES WILL FAIL TO HAVE THEIR
DESIRED EFFECTS, AND COULD EXACERBATE CURRENT PROBLEMS.

Harvard Business School professor Regina Herzlinger, for example, writes that the key to health care reform is to let "consumers
take control":

> [I]f companies are willing to give their employees substantially enhanced choice among health plans, much greater control over how much they spend for various health care needs, and much more information to help them make the right choices . . . entrepreneurs will respond to the unleashing of consumer demands with clearly differentiated products featuring various combinations of benefits, levels of insurance coverage, payment systems for providers, lengths of policies, and sources of information. The competition among the new products, in turn, will control costs while improving the overall quality of coverage and care.[14]

Consumers are quite capable of dealing with complex purchasing decisions. There are dozens and dozens of choices of wide-screen television sets, for example, differentiated by price, technology, picture quality, service warranty, and other features. But the average shopper is skilled at narrowing choices and making selections, so superior offerings usually pretty quickly emerge as winners.

Accordingly, the Bush administration's 2003 Medicare drug discount card came with a rich menu of options from multiple competitive vendors, just as Herzlinger might have suggested. But seniors mostly passed it up, although it offered a chance for substantial savings. Field reports suggest that people simply could not deal with the fifty-plus programs offered.[15] The new Part D Medicare prescription drug program is built on the same lines. Medicare enrollees are being presented with about forty different plan options with wide variations in monthly charges, the number and type of drugs covered, rules on deductibles and copays, and so forth, again in keeping with Herzlinger's prescription.

The early days of "Medigap" insurance, unfortunately, offer a precedent that is right on point and not very encouraging. Medigap was pioneered by Colonial Penn insurance company, in partnership with the AARP, to insure against charges not covered by Medicare. (Although the AARP has long since cleaned up its act, it was originally little more than a marketing arm for Colonial Penn.) Trusting seniors signed up in droves and, according to a devastating 1976 *Consumer Reports* review, were badly ripped off. Hundreds of other private companies piled into the market with a vast range of plans, some good and some dreadful, but all so complicated that it took an insurance actuary to tell the difference. Congress finally stepped in in 1981 and mandated a limited schedule of ten different plans. Companies compete on price and service, but the offerings and offering descriptions must be identical, and there are minimum standards for revenue/benefit payout ratios. The standardized plans have been very successful; seniors understand them and readily choose between them; and the excess profits have disappeared. It took government-imposed standardization, in short, to make the market efficient.[16]

The outlook for Part D looks like a replay of the early Medigap. Goldman, Sachs analysts have estimated that the largest insurance companies will earn $250 million from Medicare prescription drug coverage in 2006,[17] while the boost to pharmaceutical company earnings will presumably help offset their billions in losses on Vioxx and other class-action suits. The $1 billion-plus that will be spent on Part D plan advertising is not a public service contribution. Companies are leaping into the fray because an opaque, inefficient Part D market has the smell of windfall profits. The profits, and all the new spending on ad agencies and media, of course, will come from the Medicare budget.

Another test for Herzlinger's forecast came when the Supreme Court opened the door to prescription drug advertising—as Justice Clarence Thomas remarked, how could one justify keeping consumers "in the dark"?[18] Among the idiocies that have followed in consequence is the Vioxx fiasco—which may actually sink Merck—and AstraZeneca's "Purple Pill," Nexium. When its patent on the antacid Prilosec expired, AstraZeneca mounted a half-billion-dollar advertising campaign to push a new drug, Nexium, at six times the price of generic Prilosec, even though the two are virtually identical and produce virtually identical results. Why would a doctor prescribe Nexium? Ask one, and he will tell you that patients come in and demand it. After all, that is why the companies spend so much on advertising—not to educate, but to push consumers toward products that doctors, on their own, probably would not recommend.

The behavior of the pharmaceutical companies is more comprehensible when they are understood as mass-market businesses, which is unusual in health care. Once a drug like Prilosec or Prozac has cleared the FDA, the global sales economics are not much different than for Coke or Pepsi. The dancing, golfing couples in Vioxx ads were almost interchangeable with soft drink ad models, while former senator Bob Dole's "little blue friend" television ad campaign for Pepsi was a hilarious spoof of his earlier ad campaign for Viagra. From the standpoint of pharmaceutical shareholders, the proliferation of "me-too" mass market drugs is as sensible, and as profitable, as proliferating me-too brands like 7-Up, Fresca, and Sprite. Nor should it be surprising—absent mass public pressure—that the companies are reluctant to spend resources on drugs with more limited, or precarious, markets, like flu vaccines (the virus is highly variable and all vaccines carry liability issues) or agents against diseases like leishmaniasis or dengue fever, which are endemic in less developed countries. (It remains to be seen how the rich-country pharmaceutical companies deal with the challenge from Indian and Chinese manufacturers, whose home countries may choose not to recognize American and European patents for drugs of high importance.)

Buying health care, at the end of the day, is not like buying television sets. It is not the affluent, healthy, probing consumer implied by Herzlinger's model that accounts for the spending.* Mostly, it is people who are sick, frightened, and not likely to be thinking clearly. You are in a hospital, festooned with stitches and tubes, and your doctor comes by to tell you about chemotherapy—do you reach for your laptop Web browser? Even if you did, the Web is not *Consumer Reports*. Much of the available health care information is dross, and quite a lot is spectacularly wrong.

A recent generation of economists has begun to face up to the realization that consumers often do not behave like the utility-maximizing rational agents hypothesized by market-economy theorists.

---

* The default market-conservative explanation—that the consumer is not putting up enough of his own money—implicitly assumes the same type of activist consumer as Herzlinger does. The cost of an episode of extreme illness, in any case, is so high that first-dollar cost barriers become irrelevant.

In the real world, people frequently face complicated choices among multiple alternatives with highly uncertain outcomes. A man is told that open-heart surgery may save his life or might kill him—what should he do? An older woman does not know what drugs she will need two or three years from now, or even next year. She is given forty drug coverage options—the first has 1,500 drugs, the second 2,500, but costs more (actual examples). Which is better? And there are thirty-eight more to analyze.

The relatively new field of "behavioral economics" tries to discover how people make choices in such circumstances. Richard Frank of Harvard University, who has a long record of creative probing at how health care works in the real world, has put the industry under a behavioral economics lens.[19] A short list of suggestive insights:

Both physicians and patients tend to behave in accord with well-known models of decisionmaking under conditions of uncertainty. They tend to rely more on sources they *trust* (for patients, it is usually family and friends first, and doctors second; for doctors, it is their practice group and immediate peers). Abstract, impersonal sources, like medical journals or physician-rating systems, are surprisingly unimportant.[*] Frank also suggests how large local practice variations build up. A doctor who decides to depart from a community norm is likely to make a considerable investment—reading journals, attending conferences, learning new methods. That level of effort may unconsciously bias her to

---

* New York state is in advance of most in providing consumer information on doctors. The state Web site includes misconduct and malpractice information, so a consumer can at least weed out a charlatan or incompetent. (But in some specialties, like neonatology, malpractice actions are routine since so many neonates die or are severely disabled, so interpreting the data is not straightforward.) Commendably, the state also publishes heart surgery death rates for both hospitals and surgeons. But almost all fall within state norms at a 95 percent confidence level. The big gains may have come in the first year. The postings apparently forced the withdrawal of the worst doctors, presumably through peer pressure. It also may have created a suboptimal practice bias toward less risky patients. Overall, the very low demand response to the ratings was a disappointment to reformers.

perceive positive outcomes, and to "sell" her peers. Vivid success anecdotes from a peer typically carry more weight than the bare-bones reports of a controlled study. Doctors, after all, tend to see patients in fifteen-minute time slots, and do not have the luxury of spending hours researching each case.

Both patients and doctors tend to make decisions in a way to minimize *regret* and the sense of *responsibility* for the wrong choice. It is natural, and safer, for physicians to give greater weight to local practice standards than to journal recommendations. For their part, patients like to leave the major decisions to the doctor. They also strongly resist changing medications and prefer first-dollar medical coverage, even when analysis shows the excess premiums are uneconomic, since it lets them make fewer decisions.

Hospitals are fairly responsive to detailed economic incentives—they have large staffs devoted to their interpretation—but physicians and patients typically are not. The average doctor's patient mix, after all, may represent fifteen or more payment plans. He is usually unsure of what coverage patients have (office staff handle the billing details), so he treats similar patients similarly, and takes pride in adhering to a "professional" standard. Patients, it turns out, rarely know the difference between one health plan and another.

While Frank's work is at an early stage, it comports well with common sense. Real health care is not the pure, neoclassical market of market-conservatives' imagination. There are at least two important implications. The first is that several decades of spinning out ever-more elaborate payment-based incentive systems has produced only oceans of paperwork—sheer economic waste. It is an absurd way to achieve best-practice medical standards. And the second implication is that, if the market theologians currently in the policy saddle have their way, the snarl is likely to become much worse.

6

THE ROCKY PATH TO REFORM

It is far easier to devise reasonable reform outcomes than it is to envision a plausible path for accomplishing them. The American system of government is not conducive to major policy reversals. Most important American reforms, like the New Deal legislation, came only after a period of profound crisis. Even the Medicare and Medicaid legislation were wrung from a skeptical Congress by dint of Lyndon Johnson's masterful exploitation of the Kennedy assassination. The Clinton-era welfare reform legislation may be an exception to that rule, but it was the product of a rare cross-party consensus that evolved over several decades.

The reforms required in American social insurance are very large and very complicated, and even where there is a rough consensus on objectives, there is hardly a glimmer of consensus on means. Nor is there more than a wisp of a chance that a group of intelligent and well-meaning people of various political hues might sit down and agree on a comprehensive approach that could be sold to the Congress and the public.

As private employers continue to shuck their old social insurance responsibilities, however, and especially as health care spending continues to spiral upward, there will be a crisis in government finance that will trigger some sort of action. What follows are not reform proposals, but merely a listing of key issues that must be addressed by an enduring reform.

PENSIONS

Gnarly as it is, the pension problem is more tractable than health care, and fits more readily within current institutional conventions. (And some economists feel that it has been consistently overstated by an asset-hungry retirement industry.) But there are still many reasons for concern. The recent collapse in savings could well jeopardize the futures of American families and open the door to a long list of other economic maladies besides.

Making progress on savings, however, would imply certain minimum essential steps:

◆   Maintaining the Social Security program in its present form, adjusted only as needed to achieve seventy-five-year Trust Fund actuarial balance. Congress should thereafter rebalance the program every ten years to bring funding and benefits into accord with the then-current forecast.

◆   Restoration of the fiscal integrity of the federal government. Given the scale of current deficits, that will certainly require a tax response, including a rollback of most or all of the Bush tax program.

◆   Limiting sub-prime lending to households and, ideally, placing some curbs on the liquidation of housing equity.[*]

◆   Increasing constraints on preretirement liquidation of IRAs, defined contribution pensions, and similar assets.

---

[*] There is an intriguing symmetry between the buildup in corporate savings in recent years and the collapse of consumer savings, especially since so many large American companies have substantial consumer lending operations. (GE's spectacular profit growth in the 1990s, for instance, was mostly driven from its lending operations.) The financial destruction of households and the recovery of the corporate sector, it is likely, are two faces of a single phenomenon.

◆ Reorienting savings incentives away from the wealthy (such as raising ceilings on tax-advantaged savings) and toward the middle and lower-middle classes.

Additional steps could include the consideration of mandatory savings deductions for all workers, possibly with government matching donations. Many academics also favor converting from a primarily income-tax revenue base to a primarily consumption-based tax regimen (which need not be regressive[1]), although it seems unlikely that the current federal tax-legislating machinery could produce a nonregressive consumption tax. Any such radical proposals would require far more analysis of their likely economic impact and cost incidence than they have received to date.

HEALTH CARE

Although health care is clearly straining its current patchwork *financing* system, the continued expansion of its share of GDP is clearly within the country's economic capacity—indeed, it may well have a number of positive consequences in terms of employment, international financial balances, and continued leadership in microelectronics and microbiology. It is critical, however, that the continued growth expansion of health care spending be accompanied by major operational and quality improvements.

FINANCING

The objective of financing reform should be to establish sustainable financing mechanisms consistent with America's mixed public-private enterprise system. A conceivable approach would include:

◆ The federal government would establish a federally regulated basic health plan that would be a minimum standard for all employees and also replace current Medicare and Medicaid. The offering would be standardized, as in Medigap, but could be sold by all qualified insurance vendors. Limits on both procedures and costs would apply, along with required copays and deductibles to help ensure efficient use of resources.

◆ Insurance companies would be free to offer supplemental coverage for basic plan enrollees, or comprehensive programs for people who want superior benefits. Only the basic plan payments would be tax-advantaged.

◆ All employers would be obligated to offer the basic plan to their employees; the insurance would be contributory for employees subject to a wage-based sliding scale. Premiums for low-wage employees, the elderly, and the poor unemployed would be subsidized by the federal government. An employer's premium for the basic plan also might be capped (subsidized) to maintain competitiveness in a global marketplace.

◆ Government subventions would be covered by a dedicated, progressive, broad-based tax. The program would therefore have substantial redistributive elements.

OPERATIONS

Doctors who wish to participate in the basic plan would join one or more physician networks, although they would be free to limit their practices to the carriage-trade unsubsidized plans. All plan-eligible physician networks would be required to comply with evolving comprehensive data exchange, electronic record-keeping, and similar standards, and to maintain protocol- and quality-oriented medical management and disciplinary systems. Real operational reform, however, would be the work of decades, and at the very minimum would require changes like the following:

♦ A substantial conversion of National Institutes of Health and related federal research dollars from disease-focused research to the development of the data and quality standards required for high-technology medicine.

♦ Development of a cadre of medical managers to develop and maintain quality systems. Managerial overhead may possibly *increase,* but the dead weight of meaningless paper shuffling would be mostly eliminated, so the net effect may be small.

♦ Development of much more powerful industry/government quality inspection and error-detection systems. It will be essential to replace the current medical malpractice system with a workers' compensation-like system based on expert inquiry.

♦ A system of industry-government review panels to monitor current therapies and technologies, establish allowability within the basic plan, and maintain best-practice protocols.

The implementation of a system like the one hypothesized above would carry two implicit premises. The first is a forthright acceptance of the increasing economic importance of health care, and a commitment to ensuring its orderly expansion. The second is a frank recognition that the freewheeling introduction of new therapies and procedures, in the circumstance of a steeply accelerating rate of technological progress, is outrunning the practical absorptive capabilities of the health care system. In effect, there would be a conscious slowing down of the pace of technological change, and a shift of priorities toward the management and quality infrastructure to ensure its efficient use.

The proposals above are merely suggestive, and the universe of reasonable variations is very large. The near-term possibility of implementing such comprehensive departures, however, is close to nil. Health care, more than pensions, appears to be careening toward a complete administrative and political debacle, the kind of crisis from which comprehensive reforms occasionally emerge.

That process would only be hastened by a serious federal fiscal crisis, which, unfortunately, is no longer a remote possibility.

There is at least an equal possibility that the current system will continue to stagger on in roughly its current state of slow, paper-ridden deterioration for a long time. Gross health care spending, however, will continue to expand toward 30 percent or so of GDP, the stream of technical marvels will keep flowing, and the government share of spending will grow apace. The real costs to the government will be masked by spreading the spending among a proliferating bestiary of inconsistent and overlapping categorical programs. And the gap between health care for the haves and for the have-nots will grow to shameful proportions.

NOTES

CHAPTER 1

1. William J. Waitrowski, "Comparing Employee Benefits in the Public and Private Sector," *Monthly Labor Review,* December 1988, pp. 3–8.

2. William J. Waitrowski, "Medical and Retirement Plan Coverage: Explaining the Decline in Recent Years," *Monthly Labor Review,* August 2004, pp. 29–36.

3. U.S. Census Bureau, "Income, Poverty, and Health Insurance Coverage in the United States: 2004," August 2005.

4. Isaac Shapiro and Nicholas Johnson, "Total Reveneus from All Levels of Government Drop to Lowest Share of Economy Since 1968," Center on Budget and Policy Priorities, January 15, 2004.

5. David Cay Johnston, "At the Very Top, A Surge in Income in '03," *New York Times,* October 5, 2005.

CHAPTER 2

1. Jacob S. Hacker, *The Divided Welfare State: The Battle over Public and Private Social Benefits in the United States* (New York: Cambridge University Press, 2002), p. 26. Except as noted, the discussion in this section follows Hacker.

2. Alfred D. Chandler, Jr., *The Visible Hand: the Managerial Revolution in American Business* (Cambridge, Mass.: Belknap Press of Harvard University Press, 1977) is the standard account.

3. Daniel Nelson, *Managers and Workers: The Origins of the New Factory System in the United States, 1880–1920* (Madison: University of Wisconsin Press, 1975) is the standard account.

4. Jacob S. Hacker, *The Divided Welfare State*, p. 119.

5. United States Bureau of the Census, *Historical Statistics of the United States, Colonial Times to 1970* (2 vols.) (Washington, D.C.: U.S. Government Printing Office, 1975).

6. Jacob S. Hacker, *op. cit.*, pp. 79, 262.

7. Ibid., p. 156.

8. There are many accounts of this experience; mine is Charles R. Morris, *The Coming Global Boom* (New York: Bantam, 1990), pp. 7–10.

9. William Clay Ford, "Driving U.S. Competitiveness," November 10, 2004, available online at http://media.ford.com/newsroom/release_display.cfm?release=19596. Ford uses a mid-range estimate of $1,000. GM's are reportedly the highest.

CHAPTER 3

1. William Adema, "Net Social Expenditure," *Labour Market and Social Policy—Occasional Papers No. 39* (Paris: OECD, August 1999).

2. *Budget of the United States, Fiscal Year 2006*, "Analytical Perspectives" (Washington, D.C.: U.S. Government Printing Office, 2005), p. 329.

3. *The 2004 Annual Report of the Board of Trustees of the Federal Old-Age and Survivors Insurance and Disability Insurance Trust Funds* (Washington, D.C.: U.S. Government Printing Office, 2005), pp. 2–5.

4. Michael Tanner, "Social Security's Tough Transition," The Cato Institute, February 2005; http://www.socialsecurity.org/pubs/articles/tanner-041214.html.

5. *The 2004 Annual Report of the Boards of Trustees of the Federal Hospital Insurance and Federal Supplementary Medical Insurance Trust Funds* (Washington, D.C.: U.S. Government Printing Office, 2005), p. 2.

6. *Budget of the United States*, "Analytical Perspectives," p. 364.

7. *The 2004 Annual Report, Federal Hospital Insurance*, pp. 6–9.

8. For an exhaustive account of the finances, earnings implications, and reporting shenanigans engaged in by big companies relative to defined benefit pensions, see the series, CreditSuisse/First Boston, "The Magic of Pension Accounting," New York, Part I, September 27, 2002; Part II, October 23, 2003; and Part III, February 7, 2005. Except as indicated, it is the source for the pension finance material in this section.

9. See, e.g., "How Wall Street Wrecked United's Pensions," *New York Times*, July 31, 2005; "Whoops! There Goes Another Pension Plan," *New York Times*, September 18, 2005; "Slouching Toward Pension Reform" *New York Times*, October 9, 2005.

10. Richard W. Johnson and Cori E. Uccello, "Can Cash Balance Pension Plans Improve Retirement Security for Today's Workers?" Urban Institute Brief Series, No. 14 (November 2002).

11. U.S. Bureau of Labor Statistics, "National Compensation Survey: Employee Benefits in Private Industry in the United States," March 2005. (Twenty-two percent of private sector employees have access to defined benefit pensions, but a small percentage does not take up the opportunity.)

12. Nannette Byrnes, "How Public Pension Promises Are Draining State and City Budgets," *BusinessWeek Online*, May 5, 2005. Pension obligation bonds were essentially an interest rate and accounting arbitrage. The bonds were obligations of the issuing authority, not of the pension funds, so they enabled an infusion of cash without increasing stated fund liabilities. It was also assumed that the liability reduction consequent on the anticipated high market returns would easily cover the issuing authority's interest obligations. Enron's off-balance sheet financing entities were based on similar logic.

13. "Reversal of Fortune: The Rising Cost of Public Sector Pensions and Other Post-Employment Benefits," Fitch Ratings Special Report (September 18, 2003); "Accounting and Financial Reporting for Postemployment Benefits Other Than Pensions: GASB's Final Standards," *Segal Bulletin* (August 2004).

14. For access rates, U.S. Bureau of Labor Statistics, "National Compensation Survey"; for rate actually participating, U.S. Bureau of Labor Statistics, "Benefit Survey" (http:data.bls.gov/cgi-bin/surveymost, an online searchable database). The percentage of employers making contributions is from the 2001 Federal Reserve "Survey of Consumer Finance"; my appreciation to Gordon MacDonald of the Retirement Security Project for furnishing them to me. According to the Ambrose

Group, Inc., which provides salary and benefit administration for a large number of mostly start-up high-tech businesses, the percentage of their companies that provide defined contribution matching contributions is very low.

15. U.S. Census Bureau, "Net Worth and Asset Ownership of Households: 1998 and 2000," *Current Population Reports,* May 2003. See especially, Tables E and F.

16. "Hewitt Study Shows Nearly Half of U.S. Workers Cash Out of 401(k) Plans When Leaving Jobs," Hewitt Associates Press Release, July 25, 2005.

17. Participation rates are from Congressional Budget Office, "Utilization of Tax Incentives for Retirement Savings—a CBO Paper," August 2003. Asset levels are from Federal Reserve, "Flow of Funds Accounts of the United States," Tables L119b, 119c, and 225i.

18. Peter Orszag and Robert Greenstein, "Toward Progressive Pensions: A Summary of the U.S. Pension System and Proposals for Reform," Pension Rights Center (2001), p. 10.

19. Elizabeth Bell et al., "Retirement Savings Incentives and Personal Savings," Tax Policy Center, December 20, 2004.

20. John Karl Scholz et al., "Are Americans Saving Optimally for Retirement," NBER Working Paper 10260 (January 2004). My thanks to Professor Scholz for responding to questions. The study is based on a survey panel, "The Health and Retirement Survey," sponsored by the U.S. Dept. of Aging and maintained by the University of Michigan. Birth cohorts enter the survey as they turn fifty; it remains to seen whether the behavior of younger cohorts deviates from the pattern Scholz and his coauthors describe.

21. U.S. Census Bureau, "Income, Poverty, and Health Insurance Coverage in the United States: 2004," August 2005, which is a point sample. The estimates for the long-term uncovered and the number uncovered at any time during a year are based on Douglas Holtz-Eakin, Director, Congressional Budget Office, "Health Care and the Uninsured," *Testimony before the Committee on Health, Education, Labor, and Pensions, United States Senate,* January 28, 2004. Eakin's analysis used 1998 data. To estimate the 2004 long-term and short-term uninsured, I applied the 1998 ratios between those quantities and the point sample to the 2004 data.

22. U.S. Bureau of Labor Statistics, "Employment Cost Index—Historical Listing," July 29, 2005.

23. U.S. Bureau of Labor Statistics, "National Compensation Survey." Trend in employee contribution requirements from U.S. Bureau of Labor Statistics, "Benefit Survey."

24. Kaiser Family Foundation, "Employer Health Benefits: 2005 Summary of Findings and Chartpack," September 2005.

25. The *USA Today*/Kaiser Family Foundation/Harvard School of Public Health, "Health Care Costs Survey—Summary and Chartpack," August 2005.

26. Joseph Doyle, "Health Insurance, Treatment, and Outcomes: Using Automobile Accidents as Health Shocks," NBER Working Paper No. 11099 (May 2005).

27. "Health Care Takes Its Toll on Starbucks," MSNBC, September 14, 2005.

28. William Clay Ford, "Driving U.S. Competitiveness," November 10, 2004, available online at http://media.ford.com/newsroom/release_display.cfm?release=19596.

29. U.S. Census Bureau, "Income Poverty and Health Insurance Coverage." The other "federal survey" mentioned in the footnote is Agency for Healthcare Research and Quality, "Employer-Sponsored Health Insurance: Trends in Cost and Access," September 2004.

CHAPTER 4

1. Except as indicated, earnings data in this section follow Census Bureau, "Income, Poverty, and Health Insurance Coverage in the United States: 2004."

2. Robert Rector and Rea S. Hederman, Jr., "Two Americas, One Rich, One Poor?: Understanding Income Inequality in the United States," Heritage Foundation Executive Summary Backgrounder No. 1791 (August 24, 2004).

3. Emmanuel Saez and Wojciech Kopzuk, "Top Wealth Shares in the United States," NBER Working Paper No. 10339, March 2004. Data downloadable from http://emlab.berkeley.edu/users/saez/.

4. Joel Friedman and Robert Greenstein, "The President's Proposal to Make Tax Cuts Permanent," Center on Budget and Policy Priorities (January 30, 2004).

5. Federal Reserve, Release Z.1, Table B.100, June 2005. Calculations by author.

6. Freddie Mac, "Cash-Out Refinancing Activity Rises in Second Quarter 2005," August 2, 2005.

7. *The Economist*, "A Home-Grown Problem," September 10, 2005.

8. Federal Deposit Insurance Corporation, "U.S. Home Prices: Does Bust Always Follow Boom?" May 2, 2005.

9. Federal Deposit Insurance Corporation, "FDIC Outlook: The U.S. Consumer Sector," December 7, 2004.

10. Dean Fouts, "The Real Story on Real Estate," *Business Week*, August 29, 2005.

11. Elizabeth Warren and Amelia Warren Tyagi, *The Two-Income Trap: Why Middle-Class Parents Are Going Broke* (New York: Basic Books, 2003), p. 51.

CHAPTER 5

1. A basic source for the underlying economic trends is Robert William Fogel, *The Escape from Hunger and Premature Death, 1700–2100: Europe, America, and the Third World* (New York: Cambridge University Press, 2004), an important book. For details, Robert A. Margo, "The Labor Force in the Nineteenth Century," *The Cambridge Economic History of the United States*, Vol. II: *The Long Nineteenth Century* (New York: Cambridge University Press, 2000), pp. 207–43 at 213–14; U.S. Dept. of Commerce, Bureau of Economic Analysis, NIPA; and "Factory Jobs Are Becoming Scarce; It's Nothing to Worry About," *The Economist*, September 29, 2005.

2. Robert E. Hall and Charles I. Jones, "The Value of Life and the Rise in Health Spending," NBER Working Paper No. 10737 (August 2004).

3. Calculation by the author from Bureau of Economic Analysis National Income and Product Accounts, Table 2.1, "Personal Income and Its Disposition," August 2005.

4. Jack Triplett at the Brookings Institution is perhaps the leading researcher on this issue. For a more recent discussion, see, for example, J. E. Triplett and B. P. Bosworth, "Baumol's Disease Has Been Cured: IT and Multifactor Productivity in U.S. Service Industries," The Brookings Institution (2002).

5. I summarize the data and sources in Charles R. Morris, *Too Much of a Good Thing?* (New York: Century Foundation Press, 1999).

6. For the workings of the "Oregon Plan," see Jonathan Oberlander et al., "Rationing Medical Care: Rhetoric and Reality in the Oregon Health Plan," *Canadian Medical Association Journal* 164, no. 11 (May 29, 2001).

7. Michael Luo, "Drug Costs Run Free under New York Medicaid," *New York Times*, November 23, 2005.

8. Malcolm Gladwell, "How to Think about Prescription Drugs," *The New Yorker*, October 25, 2004. Depression is just one of many other examples of large-scale undertreatment. See Lisa V. Rubinstein et al., "Evidence-based Care for Depression in Managed Primary Care Practices," *Health Affairs* (September/October 1999).

9. Bruce C. Vladek, "Accounting for Future Costs in Medicare," *Health Affairs*, September 26, 2005, pp. R93–R96, adds further perspective on cost-benefit accounting in health care.

10. See, for example, Allison B. Rosen, M.D. et al., "Physicians' Views of Interventions to Reduce Medical Errors: Does Evidence of Effectiveness Matter?" *Academic Medicine* 80 (2005): 189–92; Charles P. Friedman et al., "Do Physicians Know When Their Diagnoses Are Correct?" *Journal of General Internal Medicine*, 20 (2005): 334; Anne-Marie J. Audet, M.D. et al., *Physicians' Views on Quality of Care: Findings from the Commonwealth Fund National Survey of Physicians and the Quality of Care*, The Commonwealth Fund, May 2005; Christopher L. Roy et al., "Patient Safety Concerns Arising from Test Results that Return after Hospital Discharge," *Improving Patient Care* 143, no. 2 (July 19, 2005): 121–28; Anne-Marie Audet et al., "Measure, Learn, and Improve: Physicians' Involvement in Quality Improvement," *Health Affairs*, May/June 2005, pp. 843–53.

11. Charles R. Morris, *Too Much of a Good Thing?*, pp. 48–51, has a brief summary of the episode.

12. Commonwealth Fund, "Issue of the Month: Chronic Disease Management in Medicare" (June 2005).

13. Medicare Payments Advisory Commission, "Report to the Congress: New Approaches in Medicare" (June 2004).

14. Regina E. Herzlinger, "Are Consumers the Cure for Broken Health Insurance?" *Harvard Business Review*, August 5, 2002.

15. Kaiser Daily Health Report, "One Year After Creation, Medicare Drug Discount Program Falls Short of Expected Enrollment" (December 8, 2004).

16. Charles R. Morris, *The AARP* (New York: Times Books, 1996), pp. 35–37, 215–17.

17. Stephen Singer, "Insurers Must Market Confusing Rx Plans," *Associated Press*, September 23, 2005.

18. *Thompson v. Western States Medical Center*, 535 US 357 (2002) (concurring opinion).

19. Richard G. Frank, "Behavioral Economics and Health Care Economics," NBER Working Paper No. 10881 (November 2004).

CHAPTER 6

1. See, for example, Robert H. Frank, "Remedies for the Savings Shortfall," in Teresa Ghilarducci et al., eds., *In Search of Retirement Security* (New York: The Century Foundation, 2005), pp. 59–63.

INDEX

AARP and Medigap insurance, 49

Advertising and marketing of prescription drugs, 50–51

Agriculture in U.S. economy, 40

Airlines, 20, 21

American Medical Association (AMA), 8, 11

AstraZeneca, 50

Auto industry, 9, 12, 19, 20

Baby boomers, effect of aging of, 3, 29

Bankruptcy: business bankruptcy and pension obligations, 21; causes of personal bankruptcy, 28, 38

Blue Cross/Blue Shield, 9

Bush administration: on retirement savings, methods to increase, 25; Social Security reform proposed by, 16; tax cuts under, 3, 35, 36, 56

Cash balance plans, 21

Census Bureau data: on health insurance coverage, 26; on middle-income retirement savings, 23; on upper bracket's income levels, 33

Clinton-era welfare reform, 55

Colonial Penn and Medigap insurance, 49

Congressional Budget Office study on participation in tax-advantaged pension plans, 23–24

Consensus lacking for solutions, 4, 55

Consumer Bankruptcy Project, 38

Consumer debt: reform to address, 56; trends in, 4, 36–38, 56

Consumer Reports on Medigap insurance, 49–50

Consumer spending patterns, 41

Consumption-based tax, 57

CreditSuisse/First Boston (CSFB) on companies with pension liabilities exceeding company's market value, 20

Defined benefit pension plans, 2–3, 18–22

Defined contribution pension
    plans, 22–25, 56
Delphi (auto parts maker), 21
Delta Airlines, 20, 21
Demographic changes, 3, 29

Eisenhower administration, 10
Employee Retirement Income
    Security Act (ERISA), 19
Employer-sponsored health insur-
    ance: costs of, 27; history of,
    8–9; levels of, 28; reform,
    58; retiree liability, 12; as
    social insurance, 13
Employer-sponsored pensions:
    defined benefit plans, 2–3,
    18–22; defined contribution
    plans, 22–25, 56; forced
    retirements and, 12; history
    of, 8–9; and job change,
    22–23, 24; reform to place
    preretirement liquidation
    constraints on, 56; as social
    insurance, 13

FDA system's shortcomings, 46
FDIC on mortgage financing, 37
Federal employees and defined
    benefit plans, 22
Federal revenue loss under Bush
    administration, 36, 56
Folsom, Marion, 9, 10
Ford, William Clay, 28
401(k) plans. See Defined contri-
    bution pension plans
Frank, Richard, 52, 53
Freddie Mac on home refinanc-
    ing, 37

General Electric, 8; and profit
    from lending operations, 56
General Electric HealthCare, 42

Global environment, changes due
    to, 2, 11–12
Goldman, Sachs on Medicare
    Part D profits, 50
Government employees and
    defined benefit plans, 22
Government matching donations
    for worker savings, 57

Hacker, Jacob, 7
Health care costs, 4, 39–53; and
    decisionmaking models,
    52–53; financing reform,
    57–58; and lack of care
    coordination, 47–48; and
    life span increase, 45; and
    lobbying, 45–46; misconcep-
    tions about, 39, 40–42; and
    quality control problems,
    46–48, 59; reform based on
    consumer choice, 48–53;
    skew of benefits toward
    higher earning workers,
    43–44; and technological
    advances, 42–43, 46–47, 59.
    See also Employer-spon-
    sored health insurance;
    Medicaid; Medicare
Health care job market, 42
Health care reform, 57–60
Herzlinger, Regina, 48–49, 50, 51
History of U.S. benefit system,
    7–12
Hospital treatment: and eco-
    nomic incentives, 53; of
    insured vs. uninsured
    patients, 28
Household income trends, 31–34
Housing and lending, 37–38, 56

IBM and cash balance plan, 21
Income tax reform, 57

Income trends, 31–34
International comparison of costs of social insurance, 13–15
IRAs, 24, 56
IRS on gains of higher-income household, 35

Job change or loss: and consumer debt, 38; and employer-sponsored pensions, 22–23, 24
Job market in health care professions, 42
Johnson administration, 11, 55

Kaiser Family Foundation survey on health insurance costs, 27
Kaiser Permanente's management system, 48

Labor Department data: on defined contribution pension plans, 22; on employer-provided health insurance, 29
Life spans, effect of increase in, 45
Lobbying and health care costs, 45–46

Manufacturing in U.S. economy, 2, 7–8, 40
Marketing of prescription drugs, 50–51
Matching donations from government for worker savings, 57
Medicaid: cost of, 18; coverage of, 13, 18; drug spending in New York, 45; establishment of, 2, 11, 55; expansion of, 4; funding of, 18; Oregon Plan and care rationing, 44; reform, 58
Medical malpractice, 48, 59
Medicare: cost of, 18; drug dis-

count cards, 49; establishment of, 2, 11, 55; and lack of care coordination, 47; and Medigap insurance, 49–50; Part A (hospital coverage), 17; Part B (physician care coverage), 17; Part D (prescription drug coverage), 4, 18, 28, 46, 49, 50; reform, 58; scope of, 13
Medigap insurance, 49–50
Merck's Vioxx, 48, 50
Merrill Lynch on housing-related activities and GDP growth, 37
Mortgages, 37–38

National health insurance, 10, 28, 57–58
New Deal legislation, 9–10, 55
New York: and consumer information on physicians, 52; and Medicaid drug spending, 45
Nexium, 50
Nixon administration, 11
Northwestern Airlines, 21

Oregon Plan and health care rationing, 44
Oregon prescription drug program, 44–45

Partisan politics, 3, 4, 55
Payroll taxes used to fund Social Security, 16
Pension Benefit Guarantee Corporation (PBGC), 19, 20–21
Pensions. *See* Employer-sponsored pensions; Private pension system; Social Security

Personal debt. *See* Consumer
    debt
Personal savings: drop in, 36; by
    households, 25; incentives
    for, 57
Physician practice models, 47,
    48, 52–53; reform of, 58–59
Prescription drugs: advertising
    and marketing of, 50–51;
    FDA system's shortcomings,
    46; Medicare Part D pro-
    gram, 4, 18, 28, 46, 49, 50;
    Oregon program, 44–45;
    overseas manufacturers of,
    51
Prilosec, 50
Private health insurance, 2–3,
    26–28. *See also* Employer-
    sponsored health insurance
Private pension system: assump-
    tions about, 2; and bank-
    ruptcy of companies, 21;
    defined benefit plans, 2–3,
    18–22; defined contribution
    plans, 22–25, 56; history of,
    10; investments of, 19–20;
    reform of, 56–57. *See also*
    Employer-sponsored pensions
Privatization of Social Security, 16
Progressive initiatives, 8

Reform recommendations,
    55–60; consumer choice and
    health care costs, 48–53;
    health care, 57–60; pension
    system, 56–57

Savings. *See* Personal savings;
    Private pension system
SCHIP (State Children's Health
    Insurance Program), 28
Schultz, Howard, 28

Seriously ill and health care
    resources, 47
Six Sigma programs, 47
Small businesses and health
    insurance, 27
Social insurance, costs of, 13–15;
    reforms needed for, 55
Social Security: costs compared
    to Medicare and Medicaid,
    18; current state of, 16–17,
    25; establishment of, 9–10;
    indexed benefits, 11; reform
    of, 56–57; Trust Funds for,
    16–17
Starbucks and employee health
    insurance, 28
State and local government
    employees and defined bene-
    fit plans, 22
Steel industry, 9, 12, 20
Super-rich and income growth,
    34–36
Swope, Gerard, 9

Tax cuts of Bush administration,
    3, 35, 36, 56
Tax deductions, 9, 14, 25, 58
Taxes to fund Social Security, 16
Tax reform, 56, 57, 58
Technological advances of health
    care, 42–43, 46–47, 59
Thomas, Clarence, 50
Total Quality Management pro-
    grams, 47
Truman administration, 10
Trust Funds for Social Security,
    16–17
*The Two-Income Trap: Why
    Middle-class Parents Are
    Going Broke* (Warren &
    Tyagi), 38
Tyagi, Amelia, 38

Uninsured workers, 3, 26–27, 28
Unions and worker benefits, 9, 10
United Airways, 20, 21
U.S. Steel. *See* Steel industry

Vioxx, 48, 50, 51

Warren, Elizabeth, 38
Wealth gap, 3–4, 33–36

Welfare capitalism: assumptions about, 2; breakdown of, 29; development of, 8; negative effect of, 12; peak of, 10–11
Women and income, 32

Xerox and cash balance plan, 21

ABOUT THE AUTHOR

Charles R. Morris has many highly praised books to his credit, including *Computer Wars, American Catholic,* and *The Tycoons: How Andrew Carnegie, John D. Rockefeller, Jay Gould, and J. P. Morgan Invented the American Supereconomy.* His previous Century Foundation books include *Money, Greed, and Risk: Why Financial Crises and Crashes Happen* and *Too Much of a Good Thing? Why Health Care Spending Won't Make Us Sick.* He has published opinion pieces in the *New York Times,* the *Wall Street Journal,* the *Atlantic,* the *New Republic, Harvard Business Review,* and the *Los Angeles Times.* His wide-ranging career experiences include: managing partner of Devonshire Partners, a consulting firm; group executive at Chase Manhattan Bank; secretary of health and human services for the state of Washington; and assistant budget director for New York City.